GCSE

INFORMATION AND COMMUNICATION TECHNOLOGY

P.Evans B.Sc. (Hons)

Published by

PAYNE-GALLWAY
PUBLISHERS LTD

26-28 Northgate Street, Ipswich IP1 3DB
Tel: 01473 251097 • Fax: 01473 232758
E-mail info@payne-gallway.co.uk

www.payne-gallway.co.uk

Acknowledgements

I would like to thank everyone at Payne-Gallway Publishers for their assistance and hard work during the preparation of this text. Special thanks go to Nick Wheat for his continued support and advice.

I am grateful to the Assessment and Qualifications Alliance (AQA) for permission to use questions from their past examination papers. The sample answers provided in the teacher's supplement are the sole responsibility of the author and have neither been provided nor approved by the Assessment and Qualifications Alliance.

I would also like to thank the following organisations and individuals for permission to reproduce copyright material in the form of photographs and artwork:

Stone Computers Ltd; figure 1.5 • NASA Ames Research Centre; figures 1.4, 6.7, 16.4, 16.5 • Lilian Davies; figure 2.2 • G. Campbell, The Landbee Collection; figure 12.1 • Janet Vaughan; figure 17.4 • Flora Heathcote, figures 21.1, 21.5 • 3G Newsroom.com; figure 21.3 • The Information Commissioner; figure 23.1 and extracts from the Data Protection Act reproduced in Chapter 23 • RG Networks; figure CS 2.3 • O2; figures CS 2.1, 2.2a, 2.2b • Cross Match Technologies Inc; figure CS 2.4 • Tom Vincent, University of Bath; figure CS 3.1

Graphics: Direction123.com and Richard Chasemore

Cover picture © "Moorland Sky" reproduced with the kind permission of Gail Harvey

Cover photography © Mike Kwasniak, 160 Sidegate Lane, Ipswich

Design and artwork by Direction123.com

First edition 2000
Second edition 2001
Reprinted 2002, 2003
Third edition 2004

A catalogue entry for this book is available from the British Library.

ISBN 1 904467 54 7

Printed in Malta by Gutenberg Press

Preface

The aim

The aim of this book is to provide a clear and concise text covering all the necessary topics for a full GCSE course in Information and Communication Technology.

The chapters

The book consists of 24 chapters and four case studies covering all the essential material for a typical GCSE Information and Communication Technology scheme such as Specification A from the Assessment and Qualifications Alliance (AQA). Within each chapter there is sufficient material for one or two lessons along with a range of questions including some from recent past examination papers. Extension work is provided at the end of each chapter through a set of related web tasks.

The answers

Answers to all the questions, MS PowerPoint presentations covering the main points of each chapter, an html file containing the Website URLs listed throughout the text and advice on preparing GCSE coursework are available on the publisher's website at **www.payne-gallway.co.uk**.

Contents

Computers are **information processing machines**. They **process data** to produce **information**. The most common mistake made by people when they talk about computers is to believe they are intelligent 'thinking machines'. This could not be further from the truth. Every computer must be told exactly what to do and how to do it by a human. The instructions humans give computers are called **programs** or **software**. Without software to tell them what to do, computers would be useless.

Fig 1.1 A designer working on a personal computer

Some of the reasons for using computers are:

- computers can work much faster than humans
- computers never get tired or need a rest
- computers can do jobs that it would be dangerous for a human to do
- computers can store large amounts of information in a very small space
- computers can find information very quickly
- computers never lose or misplace information.

Input, processing and output

Whenever a computer is used, it must work its way through three basic stages before any task can be completed: input, processing and output.

A computer works through these stages by 'running' a program. A program is a set of step-by-step instructions which tells the computer exactly what to do with input in order to produce the required output.

INPUT

The input stage of computing is concerned with getting the data needed by the program into the computer. **Input devices** are used to do this. The most commonly used input devices are the **mouse** and the **keyboard**.

PROCESSING

The program contains instructions about what to do with the input. During the processing stage the computer follows these instructions using the data that has been input. What the computer produces at the end of this stage, the output, will only be as good as the input. In other words, if garbage has been input, garbage will be output. This is known as **GIGO**, or **'garbage in, garbage out'**.

OUTPUT

The output stage of computing is concerned with producing processed data as information in a form useful to the user. **Output devices** are used to do this. The most commonly used output devices are the screen, which is also called a **monitor** or **visual display unit (VDU)**, and the **printer**.

Data and information

Data is any collection of numbers, characters or other symbols that has been coded into a format which can be input to a computer and processed. Data on its own has no meaning or context. A computer processes data and turns it into useful information. For example, the string of numbers 13568180320003600 has no meaning. It is the correct processing of this data by the computer that transforms it into the information that "Employee number 13568 worked 36 hours in the week ending March 18th 2000". Exactly the same numbers processed in a different way could produce the information that "Student number 135 scored 68,18,3,20,0,36 and 0 in the last 7 tests".

In the examination you could be asked to explain what is meant by the terms data and information. Make sure you can:

- *explain what each of these terms means – a key point to include in your answer is that data has no meaning whereas information does have a meaning or context;*
- *give some examples of data and information.*

TIP

Data types

There are many **types** of data. The main types of data that can be input into a computer and processed are **numeric, text, dates, graphics** and **sound**. Data can be input to a computer by the user in many different ways. Every type of data ends up being stored as a series of numbers inside a computer.

NUMERIC

Numeric data types are split into two different sorts. The first is **integer**, a whole number which has no decimal point in it. The second is **real**. A real number is one with a decimal point in it. In both cases the symbols **0, 1, 2, 3, 4, 5, 6, 7, 8, 9** are used to represent the numbers.

TEXT

Text data includes any character on the keyboard. Text data types are also called **string**.

GRAPHICS

Diagrams, pictures and scanned images can be stored on a computer in special **graphics** files.

DATES

Dates are often treated as a kind of data on their own and stored inside the computer in a special way that makes them easier to process.

SOUND

Any sound can be recorded and stored in digital form on a computer.

The parts of a computer

Hardware is the name given to any part of a computer you can actually touch. An individual piece of hardware is called a **device**. The basic hardware of any computer consists of a **central processing unit (CPU)** and main memory together with **input, output** and **backing storage** devices. Any part of a computer other than the CPU and main memory can also be referred to as a **peripheral** device.

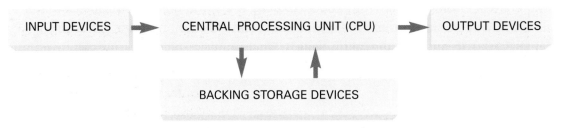

Figure 1.2 The parts of a computer

The Central Processing Unit (CPU)

The **Central Processing Unit (CPU)** is the part of a computer where the searching and sorting of data, calculating and decision-making goes on. The CPU is sometimes described as the 'brain' of the computer but this isn't really true because computers aren't able to think for themselves. The CPU contains the **Main Memory**, the **Control Unit** and the **Arithmetic and Logic Unit (ALU)**. The Main Memory holds the program instructions and data. It contains two types of memory chip, called **ROM** and **RAM** (the meaning of these terms will be explained later). The Control Unit fetches instructions from the main memory, decodes them and causes them to be executed by the ALU. The ALU performs calculations and makes decisions using these instructions.

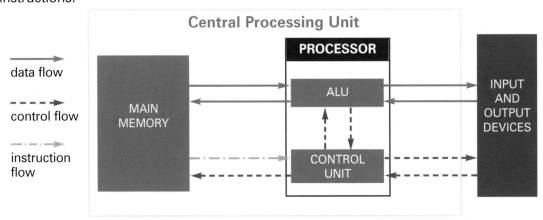

Figure 1.3 The movement of data and instructions inside the CPU

Types of computer

There are many different types of computer available today. These range from giant supercomputers to small hand-held electronic personal organisers. Some of the main types of computers in use today are described below.

Mainframe computers

Mainframe computers cost millions of pounds to buy and install. They can process extremely quickly massive amounts of data, which is stored on hundreds of disk drives. A mainframe can have hundreds of terminals (and users) connected to it at the same time. The most powerful mainframes are called **supercomputers**. Examples of organisations that use mainframes include the DVLA who use one to store data about all of the drivers and cars in the country, and the television licensing authority who use one to store data about all the households with a TV licence and everyone who buys a new television. ATM machines all over the country are linked to bank and building society mainframes, which store data about every customer and their account transactions and balances.

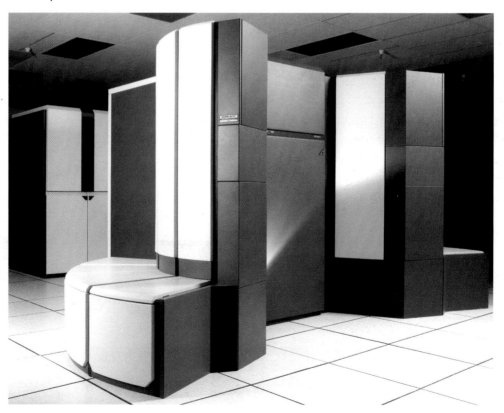

Figure 1.4 A Cray mainframe computer

Minicomputers

Minicomputers cost tens of thousands of pounds to buy and install. They are much more powerful than microcomputers but not as powerful as mainframes. Medium-sized businesses use minicomputers to control their company network and act as a central store for all the company's data.

Microcomputers

The microcomputer is the most common type of computer. Microcomputers are used in the workplace, schools and homes. Microcomputers are usually called **desktop personal computers** or **desktop PCs**.

A typical desktop PC system consists of:

- a **base unit**, or **tower unit**, that contains a CPU and backing storage devices (normally a floppy disk drive, a hard disk drive and CD-ROM or DVD-ROM drive);

- **input devices**, normally a mouse and keyboard;

- **output devices**, typically a screen, printer and speakers.

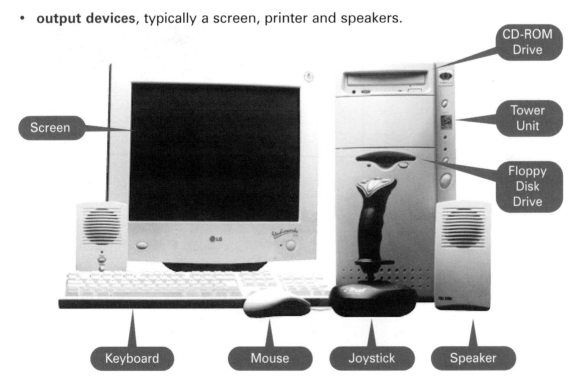

Figure 1.5 The parts of a personal computer

Portable computers

Portable computers are smaller than desktop PCs and can be easily carried around. The most common type of portable computer is the **laptop** which, as the name suggests, will fit comfortably on a user's lap. Other types of portable computer include **palmtops** and **Personal Digital Assistants (PDAs)**; these are much smaller than laptops and will fit in a shirt or jacket pocket. PDAs typically offer users facilities such as a calendar, diary, address book and, in many cases, access to e-mail and the Internet. These facilities allow users to manage their schedules and messages without the need to carry their laptop computer around. Both palmtops and PDAs can be linked to a user's laptop allowing data to be synchronised so that it is the same on both devices.

Figure 1.6 A laptop computer connected to a PDA

Questions

1. Describe what happens during each of the stages of computing listed below.
   - (a) **Input** (2)
   - (b) **Processing** (2)
   - (c) **Output** (2)

2. Draw and label a diagram to show the parts of a personal computer. (6)

3.
   - (a) Explain what is meant by the term data. (2)
   - (b) Explain what is meant by the term information and give an example. (2)
   - (c) Tick **one** box next to each item in the table below to show whether it is data or information.

	DATA	INFORMATION
(i) 04022002		
(ii) 4th February 2002		
(iii) it is a sunny day		
(iv) day a it sunny is		

   (4)

   AQA (NEAB) 2002 Paper 2 Tier H

4. Give **one suitable data type** for each item listed below.
   - (a) Date of birth (1)
   - (b) Height (1)
   - (c) Town of birth (1)
   - (d) Shoe size (1)
   - (e) Gender (1)

5. Every computer contains a **CPU** and **main memory**.
   - (a) What do the letters CPU stand for? (1)
   - (b) Why does a computer need a CPU? (2)
   - (c) Give **two** types of **memory chip** found in main memory. (2)
   - (d) Why does a computer need main memory? (2)

Web tasks

1. Visit the Free On-Line Dictionary of Computing (FOLDOC) at:
http://wombat.doc.ic.ac.uk/foldoc/

    (a) Look up definitions of the keywords highlighted in this chapter.

    (b) Prepare a summary list of keywords and definitions to use later for revision.

2. Visit **www.ai.mit.edu/people/minsky/papers/ComputersCantThink.txt**

    (a) Read the article "Why people think computers can't".

    (b) Prepare a summary of the article.

3. Visit the computer history museum at **www.computerhistory.org/**

    (a) Research the history of computers.

    (b) Construct a timeline to summarise what you find out.

4. Take a tour of Carl Friend's minicomputer museum at:
http://users.rcn.com/crfriend/museum

5. In 1997 the IBM supercomputer Deep Blue played a chess match with the world chess champion Gary Kasparov and defeated him.

    Read about this match at **www.chess.ibm.com**

Input devices are used to put data and instructions into a computer. There are two main types of input device – **direct** and **manual**.

Direct input devices can input large amounts of data quickly and accurately without any need for human intervention. **Barcode readers** and **optical mark readers** are examples of direct input devices. These and other common direct input devices and methods are described in the next chapter.

Manual input devices are used by people to enter data by hand. The most commonly used manual input devices are the **mouse** and the **keyboard**. This chapter describes these and other commonly used manual input devices.

Keyboard

The keyboard is the most common type of input device. Ordinary computer keyboards have their keys arranged in a similar way to those on a typewriter. This way of arranging the keys is called **QWERTY** because of the order in which the keys appear on the first row of letters. This layout was originally designed to separate common letter-pairs, in order to prevent nearby type-bars on a manual typewriter jamming the mechanism when typing at speed. Keyboards are now available with different layouts designed help users type more quickly and comfortably. Computer keyboards also have extra **function keys** which can carry out different tasks depending on the software being used.

Figure 2.1 A QWERTY keyboard layout

Concept keyboards

A concept keyboard is a flat board with a grid of programmable keys on its surface. A single key or a group of keys can be set up to carry out a particular task. Paper overlays are placed on top of the keyboard with pictures drawn on them to represent what will happen if the keys in a certain position are pressed. Concept keyboards are often used with young children in primary schools who can't use an ordinary keyboard very well.

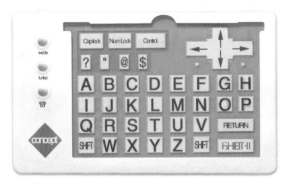

Figure 2.2 A concept keyboard

Some computer keyboards have a completely different set of keys and layout because of the special tasks that they have been designed for. The keys on the keyboard of a supermarket till are a good example of this – just take a look at them next time you go shopping!

Mouse

A mouse is a **pointing device**. It is the next most common type of input device after the keyboard. A mouse is moved around by the user on a flat surface next to the computer. When a mouse is moved, a small ball underneath it turns. The mouse detects which way the ball is turning and sends data about this to the computer.

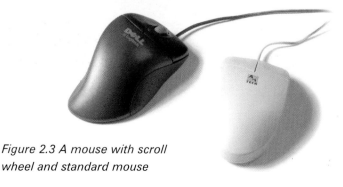

Figure 2.3 A mouse with scroll wheel and standard mouse

An increasingly popular type of mouse is the **optical mouse**. An optical mouse works by taking hundreds of pictures each second of the surface it is resting on and analysing them for any changes. The distance and direction the mouse has moved is worked out from differences in the pictures by a processor inside the mouse. Information about the movement of the mouse is then sent to the computer as a set of coordinates.

Figure 2.4 The underside of an optical mouse

Special '**mouse driver**' software uses data from a mouse to move a small **cursor arrow** around the screen. Once the user has used the mouse to point the arrow on the screen at something, it can be selected by clicking a button on top of the mouse. Every modern mouse has at least two buttons on it. The left-hand button is the one that is normally used to make selections.

Touch pads and **trackballs** are also types of pointing device. They are often used instead of a mouse on portable computers.

Figure 2.5 A touch pad being used instead of a mouse on a laptop computer

Joystick

The main use of a joystick is to play computer games by controlling the way that something moves on the screen. Joysticks can be used to control movement from side-to-side, up-and-down and diagonally. A joystick will also always have at least one button on it which can be used to make something happen like making a character in a game jump or fire a gun.

Figure 2.6 A joystick

Touch screen

A touch screen can detect exactly where on its surface it has been touched. There are several ways in which this can be done. One common type of touch screen uses beams of invisible infra-red light which shine from top-to-bottom and side-to-side just in front of the screen. The beams of light form a grid that divides up the screen. When the screen is touched some of the beams are blocked and the exact position where the screen has been touched can be worked out by the computer. Touch screens are used in a lot of restaurants because they are easy to keep clean and re-program when changes are made to the menu.

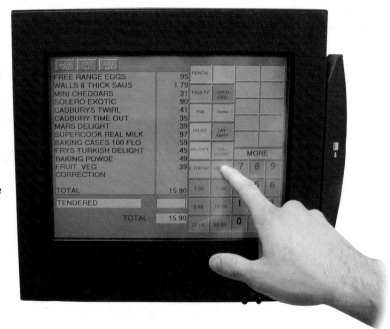

Figure 2.7 A touch screen in operation at a store checkout

Scanner

A scanner can be used to input pictures and text into a computer. There are two main types of scanner; **hand-held** and **flat-bed** scanners work by passing a beam of bright light over an image. Data about the amount of light reflected by the different parts of the picture is collected by sensors inside the scanner.

Figure 2.8 A flat-bed scanner

This data is used to produce a digital image of the picture that the computer can display on the screen. Once the image has been scanned it can be saved and changed using special software. If text has been scanned, special **optical character recognition** software must be used to convert the digital image into real text.

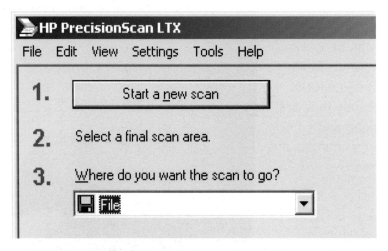

Figure 2.9 OCR scanning software being used to scan a page of printed text

Digital camera

A digital camera can store many more pictures than an ordinary camera. The number of images a digital camera can store depends on the memory space available inside the camera and the **resolution** of the images being stored (this will be explained later). Pictures taken using a digital camera are stored inside its memory and can be transferred to a computer by connecting the camera to it. This avoids the need to buy film, pay for it to be developed and wait for the pictures to come back. If you take a picture with a digital camera you can view the result straight away and take another one if you're not satisfied with it.

Figure 2.10 An Epson digital camera

Pictures taken using a digital camera are already in electronic format. This offers users a number of advantages compared with using ordinary photographs. The most important advantage of digital images is that they can be used straight away in other programs such as word-processors or desktop publishing packages, whereas ordinary pictures would have to be scanned first. Digital photographs can also be transferred easily between computers, either on disk or across the Internet, and they can be edited to change their size and appearance using special graphics software.

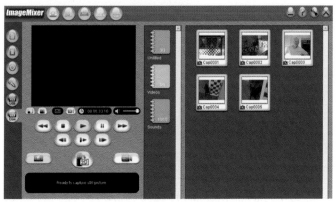

Figure 2.11 Special software being used to retrieve some pictures from a digital camera and save them on the hard disk drive of a PC

A digital camera takes pictures by converting the light passing through the lens at the front into a digital image. It does this by using a grid of tiny light sensors which convert the light that is falling on them into **binary patterns** of 0s and 1s. Different binary patterns are used to represent the different colours and shades of light that make up a picture. Some digital cameras can also capture short clips of moving images. For longer video clips a digital video camera is needed. Digital video cameras can be connected directly to a computer using a special **firewire cable** which allows video to be saved to the hard disk drive and edited using special software.

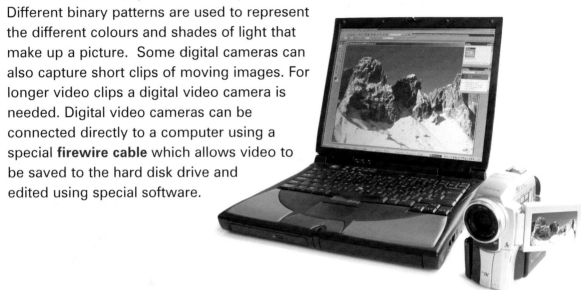

Figure 2.12 A digital video camera connected to a laptop computer

Web cams are another common type of digital camera. Web cams can take photographs and capture moving images which can be saved on the computer they are connected to or transmitted across the Internet.

Figure 2.13 A web cam connected to a PC

Graphics tablet

A graphics tablet consists of a flat surface and a pen, or **stylus**, which can be used to produce freehand drawings or trace around shapes. When the stylus touches the surface of the graphics tablet, data about its position is sent to the computer. This data is used to produce on the screen an exact copy of what is being drawn on the surface of the graphics tablet.

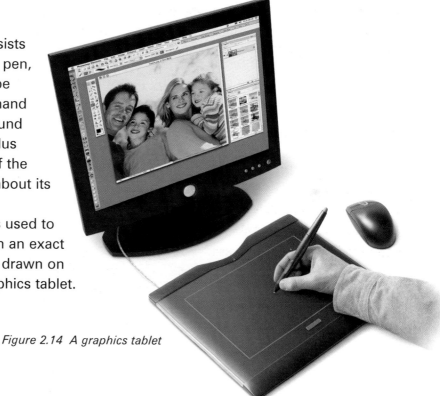

Figure 2.14 A graphics tablet

Microphone

A microphone is used to input sound into a computer system. Microphones are often used for voice recognition systems, which convert sounds made by a user into text on the screen or commands the computer can carry out. Systems like this are very useful for people who can't use ordinary input devices such as the mouse and keyboard. As computers become more powerful in the future, voice recognition will be a much more common input method for all computer users.

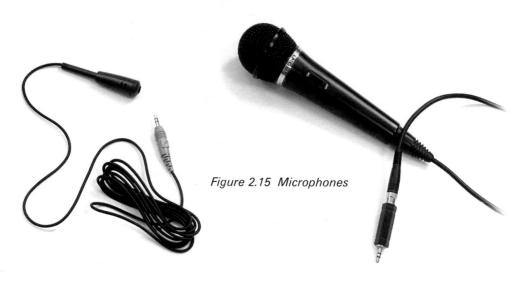

Figure 2.15 Microphones

Light pen

A **light pen** is a small 'pen-shaped' wand, which contains light sensors. The light pen is used to choose objects or commands on the screen, either by pressing it against the surface of the screen or by pressing a small switch on its side. This sends a signal to the computer, which then works out the light pen's exact location on the screen. The advantage of a light pen is that, unlike a 'touch screen', it doesn't need a special screen or screen coating.

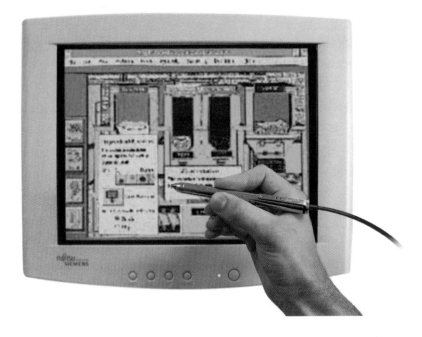

Figure 2.16 A light pen

TIP

In the examination you could be asked to suggest the most suitable input devices for a variety of different tasks.

For each input device described in this chapter make sure that you know:

* *how it is used;*
* *what sort of tasks it is used for.*

Questions

1. Tick **five** boxes to show which of the following are **input** devices.

	Tick **five** boxes only
Touch sensitive screen	
Plotter	
Motors	
CD-ROM	
Speaker	
Graphics digitiser	
VDU	
ROM	
DTP package	
Light pen	
Microphone	
Sensor	
RAM	

(5)

AQA (NEAB) 1999 Paper 1 Tier F

2. (a) Explain what is meant by the term manual input device. (2)

(b) Give three examples of manual input devices. (4)

(c) Give one possible disadvantage of using a manual input device. (1)

3. For each of the tasks listed below give one suitable type of input device.

(a) Entering a customer's order at the till in a fast food restaurant.

(b) Transferring a page of printed text into a word processing program.

(c) Teaching very young children about computers in a primary school.

(d) Taking pictures of a school for its website.

(e) Pointing and clicking on options on a computer screen.

(f) Converting an old map into a digital format.

(g) Typing a report into a word processing program. (7)

4. One of your friends is considering buying a new personal computer (PC) and has asked for your advice about the *input devices* she will need.

    (a) Give **two** input devices that your friend should expect to receive as part of any standard PC package. You should explain briefly why each of these devices is needed. (4)

    (b) Give **two** other input devices which it might also be useful for your friend to consider buying. In each case explain carefully why your friend should consider the extra expense of having these input devices as well. (4)

Web Tasks

1. Visit the Free On-Line Dictionary of Computing (FOLDOC) at:
    http://wombat.doc.ic.ac.uk/foldoc/

    (a) Look up definitions of the keywords highlighted in this chapter.

    (b) Prepare a summary list of keywords and definitions to use for revision.

2. Use the PC Technology Guide at **www.pctechguide.com** to find out more about the input devices described in this chapter.

3. Use **www.google.co.uk** to find advice about the features to look out for when buying a digital camera. Use the information you find to prepare a one-page guide on buying a digital camera for an adult who recently bought their first computer.

4. Visit **http://florin.stanford.edu/~t361/Fall2000/TWeston/home.html**

    (a) Carry out some research about voice recognition technology.

    (b) Prepare a short presentation for the rest of the class that answers these questions:

    • What can today's technology do?

    • How does it work?

    • What might tomorrow's technology do?

The last chapter described manual input methods, which are used by people to enter data by hand. In this chapter we will look at some methods of capturing and entering data directly without any need for human intervention. This is sometimes called **direct data entry**, or **DDE** for short, and is used when very large amounts of data need to be input quickly and accurately.

Optical mark recognition

Optical mark recognition, or **OMR**, uses an input device called an **optical mark reader** to detect marks made in certain places on specially printed forms. OMR is a fast input method used to input data from things like answer sheets for multiple-choice exams and registration forms in schools. The most common day-to-day use of OMR in the UK is to input data from National Lottery forms.

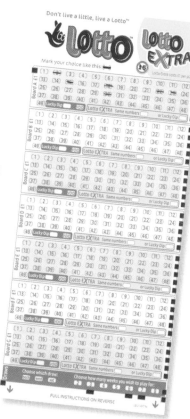

Figure 3.1 A completed lottery playslip ready to be input at a lottery terminal. OMR is used by the terminal to input the numbers from the playslip so that they can be printed on the ticket and transmitted to lottery headquarters

Magnetic ink character recognition

Magnetic ink character recognition, or **MICR**, uses an input device called a **magnetic ink character reader** to input characters that have been printed in special magnetic ink. Banks use MICR to process cheques. The numbers along the bottom of a cheque are printed in magnetic ink. When cheques are paid into a bank the staff have to type in the amounts so that they can be printed on the bottom of the cheque in magnetic ink. Cheques that have been processed in this way are sent to special cheque-clearing centres where they can be processed automatically in very large batches using magnetic ink character readers. Banks use this method of input for processing cheques because it is very secure. The equipment needed to print and read characters in magnetic ink is very expensive and it is unlikely that anyone would go to the trouble of trying to get hold of some just to forge cheques.

Figure 3.2 Characters are printed in magnetic ink at the bottom of a cheque. The groups of numbers represent the cheque number, the sort code (this identifies the branch that issued the cheque)
and the account number. The amount written on the cheque is printed on it in magnetic ink once it has been paid into a bank

Optical character recognition

Optical character recognition, or **OCR**, is the use of a scanner and special software to convert text in a scanned image into a format that can be edited by word processing software. Text that is going to be input using OCR must be printed or written very clearly because poorly shaped or unclear text won't be recognised. OCR is also used for the reading of typed postcodes when mail is automatically sorted. Payment slips accompanying credit card payments are also read using OCR. The main difference between OCR and OMR is that OCR depends on the shape of the marks whereas OMR depends on the position of the marks.

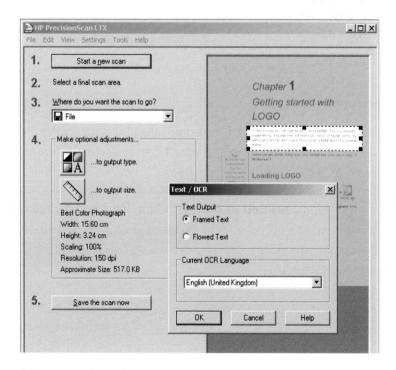

Figure 3.3 Scanning a section of printed text scanned using OCR

Barcode reader

A barcode is a set of lines of different thicknesses that represents a number. **Barcode Readers** are used to input data from barcodes. Most products in shops have barcodes on them. Barcode readers work by shining a beam of light on the lines that make up the barcode and detecting the amount of light that is reflected back. Many barcode readers use the light from a laser beam to scan the barcode, but others, such as **light pens**, use an ordinary beam of light. Barcodes don't store any information about the price of a product – they just represent a code number for it. This number can be split up into different parts that can be used to look up information about a product such as its price, size and manufacturer on a shop's computer system. It is not only shops that use barcodes; many libraries now use barcodes on their books and membership cards.

Figure 3.4 Scanning a barcode

Magnetic strip

A magnetic strip is just a thin band of magnetic tape similar to the tape inside a music cassette. The most common place you'll come across a magnetic strip is on the back of a credit or debit card.

Figure 3.5 A magnetic strip card

Magnetic strips are also used on identity cards and electronic key cards in hotels and businesses. Some schools register their students using identity cards with a magnetic strip on them. To register, students simply swipe their card through a magnetic strip reader. The computer identifies each student by reading the identity number from the magnetic strip on their card.

Magnetic strips can hold only a small amount of data and are very easy to copy or 'clone'. This is a major problem for credit and debit card users. In 2002 over £424 million of card fraud was committed using stolen or cloned cards. From 2004 onwards cards with magnetic strips are being replaced with smart cards which store data on a small microchip built into the surface of the card.

When users pay for goods with one of these cards they will be asked to type in a Personal Identification Number (PIN) rather than signing a paper receipt. These cards are virtually impossible to copy and without the PIN a thief would not be able to use a lost or stolen card.

Figure 3.6 Using a chip and pin card at a fast food restaurant

In the examination you could be asked to suggest the most suitable method of data capture for a variety of different tasks.

For each method of data capture described in this chapter make sure you know:

- *what sort of tasks it is used for;*
- *what advantages it offers compared with manual input methods.*

*You should also make sure you know what the letters in the terms **OMR**, **OCR**, and **MICR** stand for.*

TIP

Sensors

Computers use sensors to monitor events in the outside world. Sensors detect changes in conditions like temperature, pressure, humidity and light, and send data back to a computer through an input signal. The type of sensor you are most likely to come across every day is a **passive infrared sensor** or **PIR**, which is used by burglar alarm systems to detect movement inside or outside houses – is there a PIR in the corner of the room you're in now? This is an example of a sensor being used in a **computer-controlled system** where input from sensors is used to decide what action to take. This means that if, for example, the system was active and a PIR detected movement in a room, the alarm would be sounded. Computer-controlled systems like this will be considered in more detail later on in the book.

Figure 3.7 A PIR sensor in a house

The input signal from a sensor can be either **digital** or **analogue** depending on the condition being monitored. Data about a **physical quantity** such as temperature can have any number of different values and generates an analogue signal. For a computer to be able to process analogue signals from sensors, a device called an **analogue-to-digital converter** is needed. This device converts analogue signals into equivalent digital signals that the computer is able to process. Some sensors need to be **calibrated** before they can be used. This involves matching the readings from the sensor to an accepted scale in known units.

Figure 3.8 Converting analogue sensor signals into digital signals

Data logging

Data logging is a way of using a computer to automatically collect data over a period of time without the need for human supervision. A **data logger** is a microprocessor-controlled device to which sensors can be connected allowing data to be detected. Data loggers can either be connected directly to a computer or operate stand-alone, in which case they both capture and store data until it can be transferred to a computer.

Applications of data logging

A common use of data logging is in science experiments. Taking readings during an experiment can be time-consuming and tedious. Every experiment needs accurate measurements taking if the results are going to be of any value. Measurements taken by humans are often not accurate because instruments are not read correctly, often enough or at the right time. Data logging overcomes these problems. Experiments that use data logging need no human supervision and they can take very accurate readings, often over long periods of time, at regular time intervals. The time intervals between measurements taken by a data logger can also be much shorter than is possible for a human. Data logging in science experiments can therefore produce a much greater number of very accurate results automatically.

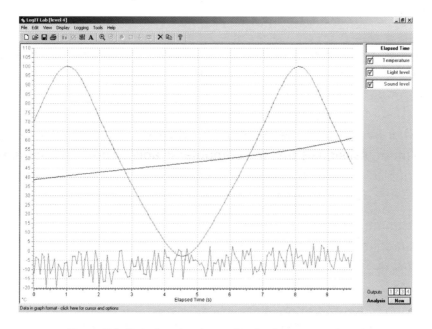

Figure 3.9 Data logging in a school science experiment

Critically ill patients need constant monitoring and this requires the full-time attention of one nurse for just one or two patients, which is often not practical or possible. Data logging can provide a solution to the problem. Patients can have their blood pressure, respiration rate, heart rate, body temperature and brain activity monitored by a data logging system. The data logger can take readings at frequent intervals and sound an alarm if any fall below a pre-set level decided upon by a doctor. As well as this constant monitoring the data logging system records the data for later analysis, which can provide an accurate and up-to-date summary of a patient's condition.

Data logging is useful when people need to collect data in remote or inhospitable conditions where it would be difficult for humans to take measurements. Automated weather-monitoring stations are used to collect data about weather conditions. Sensors are used to log and record data about physical quantities such as rainfall, wind speed, wind direction, and temperature. The data collected at each station is transferred to a central headquarters where it is combined with data from other stations to give an overall analysis of weather conditions over a large area. Collecting weather data in this way means that humans do not have to travel to locations which can often be remote and inhospitable. Data collected by these automated stations is combined with information from other sources such as satellites to produce weather forecasts.

Figure 3.10 An automated weather station

Air pollution is a growing problem, especially in our cities. Data logging can help with the monitoring of air quality. Many cities now have automated air-quality monitoring stations. These use data-logging equipment to measure and record data about physical quantities such as pollen and carbon monoxide levels.

Whatever the application is, once the data has been collected it can be transferred anywhere using communications links like satellites and telephone lines. Once the 'logged' data has been transferred it can be analysed by computers at its final destination.

The stages of data logging

The process of data logging can be broken down into a number of different stages, described below:

Stage 1

SET UP THE EQUIPMENT This might simply involve putting some apparatus together in a laboratory and connecting sensors to it. If data is being collected remotely, the site must be visited and equipment installed, including a communications link across which data can be transferred.

Stage 2

SET THE PERIOD OF LOGGING AND TIME INTERVAL The period of logging is the total time for which the data is going to be logged. The time interval is the amount of time that passes between measurements. The period of logging and the time interval chosen will depend upon the type of process which is being logged.

Stage 3

COLLECT THE DATA Readings are taken and recorded at the set time intervals throughout the logging period.

Stage 4

TRANSFER THE COLLECTED DATA TO A COMPUTER In the case of remote data logging this will be through a communications link such as a telephone line or satellite connection. If data has been collected locally, data is normally transferred through a direct connection to a computer.

Stage 5

ANALYSE THE COLLECTED DATA The collected data can be analysed in many different ways. Two of the most common methods are the use of a spreadsheet package or an application package designed for statistical analysis.

In the examination you could be asked to give some advantages of using data logging rather than traditional manual methods to gather data. Some possible answers are:

- *readings are much more accurate;*
- *data can be logged over any period of time without the need for human intervention;*
- *humans are released from boring, time-consuming and repetitive work.*

You should also make sure you can describe an application of data logging, such as collecting science data or monitoring the weather.

TIP

Questions

1. The following are different methods of data capture that can be used.

questionnaires	data capture forms	data logging
feedback	OMR	OCR
MICR	bar codes	magnetic strip

   From the list above, choose the most suitable method of data capture for each of the situations given below.

   (a) To input cheque details including the cheque number and the value of the cheque. (1)

   (b) To input students' answers to multiple-choice examination questions. (1)

   (c) To collect information about pupils' views on their new cafeteria system. (1)

   (d) To capture and store temperatures every second during a chemical reaction. (1)

   (e) To input information such as the account number from credit cards. (1)

   (f) To input information about books being taken out of a library. (1)

   AQA (NEAB) 2000 Paper 1 Tier H

2. To help increase security at their factory, Economy Electronics have decided to fit Passive Infra Red (PIR) sensors in all their storerooms.

   (a) Give **two other different** types of sensor that could be fitted to detect when a person breaks into one of the storerooms. (2)

   (b) Explain why **more than one** sensor may be needed. (2)

   (c) Explain why the sensors may need to be calibrated to a known scale before use. (2)

   AQA (NEAB) 2001 Paper 1 Tier F

3. From the list given below, choose which term best matches the definition in the left-hand column of the table which follows. Write your answers in the spaces provided in the right-hand column.

bar codes	logging interval	period of logging
calibration	magnetic strips	questionnaires
data capture forms	MICR	sensor
data logging	OCR	tabulation
feedback	OMR	

Definition	Term which best matches the definition
The collecting and storage of data at regular, fixed intervals over a period of time.	
A method of data input used in banking to read magnetised ink on cheques.	
Used to store data such as the account number and expiry date on credit and bank cards.	
The continuous checking of data from sensors to control the output of a computer system.	
A method of inputting data in which reflected light is used to detect character patterns.	
A method of matching readings from a sensor to an accepted scale in known units.	

AQA 2003 Foundation Tier

4. MICR and OCR are both examples of direct input methods.

    (a) (i) What does the term **MICR** stand for? (1)

       (ii) Give **one** application of MICR. (1)

    (b) (i) What does the term **OCR** stand for? (1)

       (ii) Give **one** application of OCR. (1)

    (c) Explain the difference between MICR and OCR. (2)

Web tasks

1. Visit the Free On-Line Dictionary of Computing (FOLDOC) at:
    http://wombat.doc.ic.ac.uk/foldoc/

    (a) Look up definitions of the keywords highlighted in this chapter.

    (b) Prepare a summary list of keywords and definitions to use for revision.

2. Read the article about weather forecasting on the UK Met. Office website at:
    www.meto.gov.uk/education/curriculum/leaflets/forecasting.html

    Prepare a one page summary about the role of ICT in weather forecasting.

3.
    (a) Visit **www.school-resources.co.uk/DataLoggingEssay.htm**

    (b) Read through the examples of where data logging is used.

    (c) Choose one example and carry out some research.

    (d) Prepare a short presentation for the rest of your class, based on your research, to describe how and why data logging is used in the example you have chosen.

The programs and data needed by computers are stored using **data storage devices**. Data storage devices are divided into two main categories; **main memory** and **backing storage**.

Main memory

When programs and data are ready to be used they are copied from backing storage into a collection of microchips inside the computer called the **main memory**. The two most common types of microchip, which together form the main memory of a computer, are called **ROM** and **RAM** (explained later).

Computers store and process data using **binary numbers**. Binary numbers are used by computers because they are very simple to make electronic circuits for. This is because a binary number is represented by a pattern of **0**s and **1**s (1 for 'on' and 0 for 'off'). A single unit in binary is called a **bit**, which stands for **bi**nary dig**it**.

Computer memory is measured in **bytes** with one byte being made up of **eight bits**. One byte can store one character, such as A, b, =, +, 2, 3, £, *. In the example below one complete byte is shown. This byte contains the binary code that is used to represent the letter A.

Figure 4.1 The eight bit binary code for the letter A

In the example below **3 bytes** have been used to store the word **CAT** in the computer's memory. One byte is needed for each letter. The bytes shown contain the binary code that represents each of the letters C, A and T.

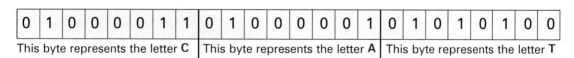

Figure 4.2 The three bytes representing the word CAT

The size of a computer's memory is normally measured in **kilobytes (Kb)**, **megabytes (Mb)** or **gigabytes (Gb)**. The table below shows some of the main units of size used to measure computer memory.

Measurement	Size (bytes)	Symbol
kilobyte	1,024	Kb
megabyte	1,048,576	Mb
gigabyte	1,073,741,824	Gb

ROM

ROM stands for **Read-Only Memory**. The programs and data stored on ROM are permanent and cannot be changed. When the computer is switched off, the contents of ROM are not lost. This sort of memory, which isn't wiped clean when the computer is turned off, is called **non-volatile memory**.

The main use of ROM memory chips in a computer is to store a program that runs when the computer is first turned on. This program loads the operating system (e.g. Windows XP) from backing storage.

RAM

RAM stands for **Random Access Memory**. RAM is the computer's 'working memory' where it stores the programs and data that are being used at any given time. The contents of RAM can be changed because it only stores programs and data temporarily. When the computer is turned off the contents of RAM are lost. This sort of memory, which is wiped clean when the computer is turned off, is called volatile memory.

Figure 4.3 RAM Memory Card

PROM and EPROM

Sometimes, when new computer systems or software are being developed, special types of read-only memory that can be programmed by the software developer are required. PROM and EPROM are both special types of programmable read only memory. **PROM** stands for **Programmable Read-Only Memory**.

Figure 4.4 An EPROM chip

This type of memory can be programmed once but can't be changed again afterwards. **EPROM** stands for **Erasable Programmable Read-Only Memory**. This type of memory can be programmed and changed whenever necessary. It is useful for, say, developing programs which will eventually be held in ROM chips inside devices like washing machines or video recorders.

In the examination you could be asked to explain what is meant by the terms ROM and RAM. Make sure you can:

- *explain the difference between these types of memory – your answer should include an explanation that RAM is volatile whereas ROM is non-volatile;*

- *explain why a computer needs both of these types of memory – your answer should mention that ROM is needed to start up the computer and RAM is needed to store programs and data currently in use.*

TIP

Backing storage

Backing storage is used to store programs and data when they are not being used or when a computer is switched off. **Magnetic tape drives, floppy disk drives** and **hard disk drives** are all examples of **backing storage devices. Hard disks, floppy disks, magnetic tapes, CD-ROMs** and **DVDs** are all examples of **backing storage media**. Backing storage devices are used to transfer data to and from backing storage media, which is what the data is actually stored on. So a floppy disk is an example of backing storage media and a floppy disk drive is an example of a backing storage device.

Hard disks

A hard disk is a circular metal disk coated with magnetic material and usually sealed in a hard disk drive inside the computer. Some hard disk drives are not permanently fixed inside the computer but are **removable**.

Data stored on hard disks can be accessed much more quickly than data stored on floppy disks. Hard disks can store much more data than floppy disks. A typical hard disk inside a personal computer can hold many gigabytes of data.

Figure 4.5 A hard disk drive

Floppy disks

A standard floppy disk is $3\frac{1}{2}$ inches wide and can store up to 1.44 Mb of data. Floppy disks are only really useful for transferring small data files between computers, such as short word-processed letters.

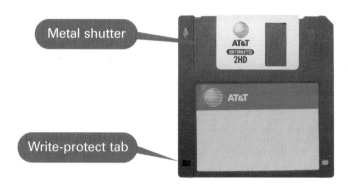

Figure 4.6 A floppy disk

An outer hard plastic cover and inner woven cloth liners protect a round plastic disk coated with a magnetic material. When the disk is put into a disk drive a metal shutter slides back revealing the surface. A small plastic write-protect tab can be clicked back to reveal a hole in the outer cover. When this tab is clicked back the disk becomes **write-protected**. This means no data can be added to or removed from the disk.

Floppy disks can be damaged quite easily if they are not treated carefully. This can result in the loss or corruption of data. Following these straightforward rules will help to protect data stored on floppy disks:

• never slide back the metal cover and touch the surface of the disk;

• keep disks away from magnetic fields — for example don't put them on top of computer monitors which generate magnetic fields;

• avoid storing disks in very hot or cold places;

• don't keep disks in damp places or allow them to get wet;

• don't bend disks;

• don't lend them to other people — they could come back with files deleted or infected by viruses;

• always label disks so that you know what's on them.

Formatting disks

Before any type of magnetic disk can be used it must be **formatted**. The process of formatting involves:

- Deleting any data that is already on the disk. Whenever a magnetic disk is formatted any data that is already on it will be permanently erased;

- Dividing the surface of the disk into invisible circles called **tracks**, which are further divided into smaller sections called **sectors**. Modern computers use high-density 3$\frac{1}{2}$ inch disks that are formatted with 18 sectors and 80 tracks on each side. One sector of a track can hold 512 bytes of data;

- Setting up a **root directory**, where the list of files that are on the disk will be kept. Data on a magnetic disk is located by finding the **address** of its location from an **index** in the root directory. Each address in the index contains a track and sector number for an individual data segment;

- Finding any bad sectors on the disk caused by damage to the disk's surface. Data cannot be stored in these areas.

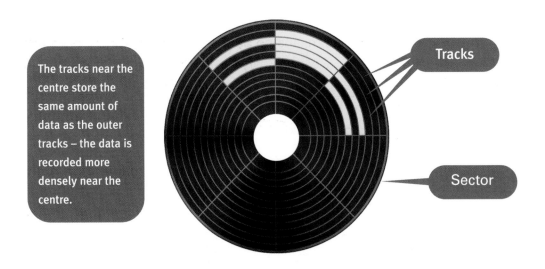

The tracks near the centre store the same amount of data as the outer tracks – the data is recorded more densely near the centre.

Tracks

Sector

Figure 4.7 A formatted disk

USB pen drives

The use of floppy disks has decreased in recent years in favour of **USB pen drives**, sometimes known as **flash memory sticks**. These devices are the size of a car key and can be plugged into the **USB port** of a PC and used just like a hard disk drive. The main advantage of pen drives is their storage capacity, which typically ranges from 32Mb up to 3Gb. Pen drives – also known as flash drives – don't need to be formatted, have no moving parts and are much more robust than floppy disks.

Figure 4.8 A USB pen drive

CD-ROM disks

CD-ROM stands for **Compact Disk Read-Only Memory**. A CD-ROM disk looks just like an ordinary music CD. CD-ROM disks can store approximately 650 megabytes of data, which is four hundred times more data than an ordinary $3^1/_2$ inch floppy disk. CD-ROM disks come with information already on them and are **read only**. This means that the information on a CD-ROM cannot be erased or changed, and no new information can be saved.

Figure 4.9 A CD-ROM disk

When a compact disk is manufactured, a laser burns small depressions called **pits** into its surface. A CD-ROM drive reads data from a disk by shining laser light onto its surface as it spins around. A sensor in the drive detects the amount of light that is reflected back from the disk's surface. No light is reflected back from the pits and these are given the binary value 0. Light is reflected back from areas where there are no pits and these are given the binary value 1. This is how data is stored on the surface of a CD-ROM as a binary pattern of 0s and 1s.

Because of their large storage capacity CD-ROMs are excellent for storing archive material. Many newspapers produce regular CD-ROM disks that contain the complete contents of their daily editions for six months or even a year. There are also many different **multimedia** encyclopaedia titles available on CD-ROM. Multimedia means that **sound**, **pictures** and **video** are all included together on the disk as well as ordinary text.

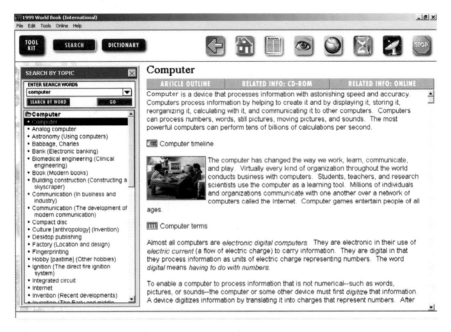

Figure 4.10 A multimedia encyclopaedia where videos, sound, animations and ordinary text are all available to the user

Writeable CD-ROM disks

Writeable CD-ROM disks are supplied blank and can have data put onto them using a special **read/write CD drive**. There are two main types of writeable compact disk; **WORM** (Write-Once, Read-Many) disks, which can have data written to them just once, and **Magneto-Optical** disks, which can have data written to them any number of times just like a hard disk.

DVD-ROM disks

The most common use of DVD-ROM disks is to store and play back feature films. DVDs are rapidly overtaking video cassette tapes as the way people watch films at home. DVD-ROM is also becoming popular as a data storage medium. The main advantage of using DVD-ROM compared with CD-ROM is its massive storage capacity: a DVD-ROM disk can store up to 17 gigabytes of data – this is over 26 times more than a single CD-ROM. Writeable DVD-ROM disks are also available and can have data put onto them using a special read/write DVD drive. New PCs are increasingly being supplied with read/write DVD drives rather than the more traditional CD-ROM drives.

Figure 4.11 Blank CD-RW and DVD-RW disks like these are quite cheap and can be used in the majority of new PCs

Magnetic tape

Magnetic tape comes in two forms; **tape reels**, and **cassettes** or **cartridges**. Large tape reels are used to make backup copies of programs and data on large mainframe computers. Cassettes like the ones used to record music were used as backing storage on early microcomputers. Cartridges are a special type of cassette that can store a large amount of data. Cartridges are used to make backup copies of the programs and data on personal computers and networks. The main advantage of using magnetic tape as backing storage is that it is relatively cheap and can store large amounts of data.

Figure 4.12 Cartridge tape

Data is stored along the length of a magnetic tape in tracks, with nine tracks being common. This gives eight data tracks and one parity track. The **parity track** is used to check that data has been correctly read from the tape.

1	0	1	Track 1
1	1	1	
0	1	1	
0	0	0	Data tracks 2
1	1	0	through 8
1	1	0	
0	0	1	
0	0	1	
0	0	1	Parity Track

Figure 4.13 Storing data on a magnetic tape

Direct and serial access

Floppy disks, hard disks, CD-ROMs and DVDs all allow direct access to data. **Direct access** means that the required data can be found straight away without having to read through all the data on the disk. This is because the address of the correct track and sector where the data is located can be found from the index on the disk. **Direct access** is also called **random access** because you can read the data back in any order — not just the order in which it was first written.

Magnetic tape allows only **serial access** to data. To locate data on a magnetic tape it has to be searched from the beginning until the required data is found. This is sometimes also known as **sequential access**. This makes it quite time-consuming to find and transfer data to and from magnetic tape compared with hard disks and CD-ROMs.

File compression

File compression is used to make files smaller so that more data can be stored in the same amount of space. It also makes it possible to send large files via the Internet more quickly, because a compressed file is much smaller than the original file. With less data to transfer, the whole process takes less time. **File compression software** is needed to compress a file. A compressed file on backing store must be **decompressed** before it can be used. This can be done using **decompression software** or by setting files up to be **self-extracting**, which means that they can automatically decompress themselves. **WinZip** is an example of software that can be used to compress and decompress files.

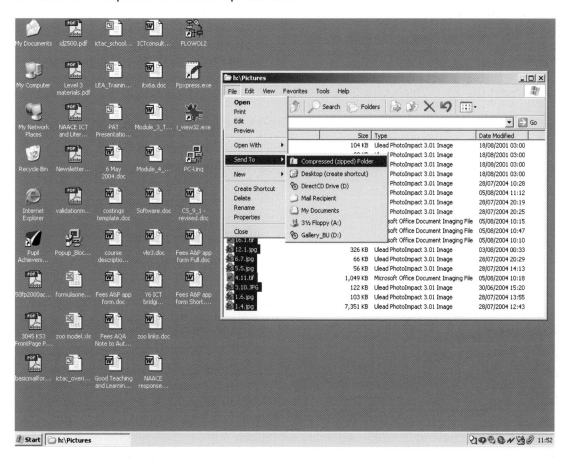

Figure 4.14 Using Windows XP to compress a collection of graphics file

Questions

1.   (a) How many bits are in one **byte**? (1)

   (b) How many bytes are needed to store one character of text data? (1)

   (c) How many bytes would be needed to store the sentence shown below? (Remember spaces count as characters as well!) (2)

   The quick brown fox jumps over the lazy dog

   (d) Sort the computer memory sizes listed below into increasing order of size with the smallest first and the biggest last.

   10Mb   100Kb   5Gb   50Mb   500Kb (1)

2. RAM and ROM are both types of memory used by personal computers.

   (a) (i) Which **one** of these types of memory is **volatile**? (1)

   (ii) Explain the difference between **volatile** and **non-volatile** memory. (2)

   (b) Why does a personal computer need both of these types of memory? (2)

   AQA 2001 Paper 2 Tier H

3. State, with at least one reason, a suitable backing storage device for each task listed below.

   (a) Storing a library of clipart pictures (1)

   (b) Making a backup copy of all the programs and data on a network (1)

   (c) Transferring work from the school network to your computer at home (1)

   (d) Saving work on your computer at home (1)

   (e) Saving a multimedia presentation (1)

4. (a) What do the letters CD-ROM stand for?   (1)

    (b) Explain what is meant by the term multimedia.   (2)

    (c) Give one reason why CD-ROMs are used to store
         multimedia applications.   (1)

    (d) Give three advantages that using a multimedia CD-ROM
         encyclopedia has over an ordinary printed version.   (3)

5.   CD-ROM   Light pen
        DVD ROM   Monitor
        DVD RAM   Mouse
        Graphics digitiser   Plotter
        Hard disk   ROM
        Keyboard   Sensor
        Laser printer   Speaker

    (a) From the list given above, choose **four** of the devices that are
         input peripherals.   (4)

    (b) From the list given above, choose **three** of the devices that
         are *output peripherals*.   (3)

    (c) From the list given above, choose **two** that are *storage media*.   (2)

                                                    AQA 2003 Foundation Tier

Web tasks

1. Visit the Free On-Line Dictionary of Computing (FOLDOC) at:
    http://wombat.doc.ic.ac.uk/foldoc/

    (a) Look up definitions of the keywords highlighted in this chapter.

    (b) Prepare a summary list of keywords and definitions to use for
        revision.

2. Prepare an illustrated set of instructions for an inexperienced user, describing
    how to compress a collection of files using Windows XP. You might like to
    start by can doing some research on this at:
    http://support.microsoft.com/

3. Visit **www.howstuffworks.com/hard-disk.htm** to find out more about how
    hard disk drives work.

Before any output can be produced by a computer it must have an **output device** connected to it. The output devices that you are probably most used to will be the **screen** (or **monitor**) and the **printer**. Another sort of output that you will have experienced when using a computer is **sound**, which is output through a **speaker**. This chapter describes the main types of devices that are used to get output from a computer.

Visual Display Unit

A **visual display unit (VDU)** or **monitor** is an output device that accepts a video signal direct from a computer. Monitors can display graphics, text and video. The size of a monitor is measured in inches diagonally across the screen; 15, 17, 19 and 21 inch monitors are the most common sizes.

Monitors can be divided into three main types: **monochrome**, **grey-scale** and **colour**. A **monochrome** monitor can display only two colours: one for the background and one for the foreground. These colours are normally black and white, green and black, or amber and black. A **grey-scale** monitor is a special type of monochrome monitor that can display different shades of grey.

Figure 5.1 A colour monitor

A **colour monitor** can display from 16 to over 1 million different colours. Colour monitors are sometimes called **RGB** monitors because they accept three separate signals - **r**ed, **g**reen and **b**lue.

The picture on a monitor is made up of thousands of tiny coloured dots called **pixels**. The quality and detail of the picture on a monitor depends on the **resolution** it is capable of displaying. Resolution is measured in pixels going across and down the screen. A **high-resolution** monitor can show much finer detail on the screen than a **low-resolution** monitor because its pictures are made up of a much larger number of pixels. Resolutions can range from 640 x 480 to 1,600 x 1,200 pixels. Most PCs are supplied with a colour 15 inch **super video graphics adaptor (SVGA)** monitor with a resolution of **1,024 x 768** pixels.

Another factor which affects the quality of the image on a monitor is its **refresh rate**. This is measured in hertz (Hz) and indicates how many times per second the image on the screen is updated. To avoid flickering images, which can lead to eyestrain and headaches, the refresh rate of a monitor should be at least 72 Hz.

Printers

A printer is an output device that produces a printout or **hard copy** of the output from a computer. There are many different types of printer available and which one you choose will depend on how much you want to pay for the printer, the cost of the paper and ink that it uses, what quality of print you want and whether you are going to print just text, graphics, or graphics and text together. The most common types of printer are **dot matrix**, **inkjet** and **laser**.

Printers can be divided into two main categories – **impact** and **non-impact**. An impact printer produces images by striking the paper. Dot matrix printers are impact printers. A non-impact printer does not strike the paper when it is printing. Inkjet and laser printers are non-impact printers.

The quality of the image produced by a printer depends on how many **dots per inch (dpi)** it is capable of printing. A printer which can produce a large number of dots per inch will produce very clear and detailed output. The speed of printers can be measured in **characters per second (cps)** or **pages per minute (ppm)** – the higher these values are, the faster the printer can produce output.

Dot matrix printer

A dot matrix printer forms characters and graphics on the paper by producing **patterns of dots**. If you look closely at a print-out from a dot matrix printer you will see the tiny dots which make up the printout. The part of the printer which forms the patterns of dots is called the **print head**. The print head is made up from **pins**, which are pushed out in different arrangements to form the various patterns of dots needed.

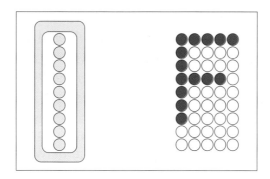

Figure 5.2 A dot matrix print head

Dot matrix printers are relatively cheap and so is the stationery that they use. Because they are 'impact printers' with the dots being printed by pins striking a ribbon against the paper, it is possible to print several copies simultaneously using two or three-part stationery. The quality of dot matrix printouts depends upon how many pins there are in the print head; a **'9-pin'** printer will produce much poorer quality printouts than a **'24-pin'** printer, for example. Dot matrix printers can be quite noisy and often need a special acoustic cover to reduce the amount of sound that they produce.

Inkjet printer

Inkjet printers work like dot matrix printers (the printouts that they produce are made up of patterns of very small dots) but the print head has a set of tiny holes rather than pins. As the print head moves across the paper, ink is forced out through the holes to form the image.

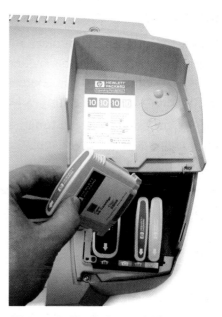

Inkjet printers are very quiet to operate and can produce good-quality printouts of both graphics and text. Relatively cheap colour graphics can be printed using a colour inkjet. Also, inkjet printers can print on different surfaces, for example printing 'sell by' dates on food containers. However, for high quality photographic images, specially coated paper is needed, which is more expensive than ordinary paper. The cost of coloured ink cartridges is also high.

Figure 5.3 Replacing an inkjet printer cartridge

Most inkjet printers have separate black and colour cartridges. The printer shown in Figure 5.3 has cartridges for black, cyan, magenta and yellow. By combining ink from the different cartridges, full colour printing is made possible. To save money, cartridges like these can be refilled using special commercially available refill kits.

Laser printer

Laser printers give very high-quality printed output of both text and graphics very quickly and quietly. Most laser printers will produce between one and twelve pages a minute. The majority of laser printers in day-to-day use can produce only black and white or **monochrome** output.

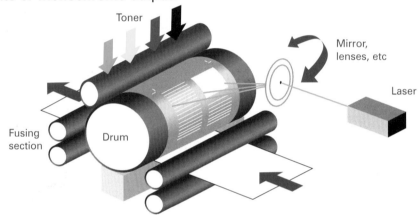

Figure 5.4 How a laser printer works

1. The **laser** is used to project an image of what needs to be printed onto a cylindrical metal **drum**. It does this by heating up the drum and creating electrical charges on its surface. Some laser printers have separate toner cartridges which do not have the drum built in. Cartridges like these can be collected and recycled.

2. Special powder, called **toner**, sticks to the charged areas on the surface of the drum creating a 'negative image'.

3. Paper is rolled around the drum and the toner sticks to it creating a 'positive image'.

4. The paper is heated, permanently fusing the toner onto it.

Laser printers are generally more expensive to buy than inkjet printers and the toner cartridges cost more, but they are very suitable for large volume printouts because of their speed. Colour laser printers are also available. They cost more than monochrome laser printers and their replacement toner cartridges are much more expensive to replace.

Figure 5.5 Replacing a toner cartridge in a colour laser printer

In the examination you could be asked to give the best type of printer to use in different situations. Make sure you know which printers:

- *are the cheapest to operate;*
- *are the most expensive to operate;*
- *produce the fastest output;*
- *produce the best quality output;*

You should justify your choice of printer for a situation based on which of these points are the most important.

Plotter

A plotter is another type of output device which will produce a hard copy of the output from a computer. The main difference between a plotter and a printer is that a plotter uses a **pen** to draw the computer output onto the paper. Some plotters use a set of coloured pens to produce colour output. Plotters produce very accurate drawings and are often used in **computer-aided design** (or **CAD**) (there is more information about this in Case Study 3).

Figure 5.6 A plotter

Speakers

Computers can output music, voices and many other complicated sounds using

speakers. To be able to output sound, a computer needs a special circuit board inside it called a **sound card**. Most PCs have at least one small speaker built into them, which generates sound from the audio input signal generated by the sound card. The quality and volume of the sound produced can be improved by connecting **external speakers** into a **port** at the back of the computer. Alternatively, headphones can be attached to this port so that the sound can only be heard by the person using the computer.

Figure 5.7 Speakers

Questions

1.   For each task listed below give the most suitable type of printer.

     (a) Printing the design for a new house, produced using a computer-aided design (CAD) package. (1)

     (b) Printing a high-quality colour copy of a photograph taken with a digital camera. (1)

     (c) Printing the first version of a word-processed letter for checking and correcting. (1)

     (d) Printing a high-quality copy of the final version of a word-processed letter. (1)

     (e) Printing invoices using two-part stationery. (1)

2.   Explain briefly what is meant by the following terms.

     (a) VDU (1)

     (b) Pixel (1)

     (c) Resolution (2)

3.   One of your friends is a keen artist. She spends a lot of time producing drawings using a PC which is getting quite old. It came with a free inkjet printer and low resolution monitor. Your friend is always complaining that her computer is no good and needs upgrading. If your friend can't afford to buy a new computer, what upgrades would you suggest she considers making to the existing system? (4)

4.   A furniture company uses a computer to help design fitted kitchens. When a customer visits the showroom a salesperson inputs their kitchen's measurements into a computer and makes suggestions about the arrangement of the various appliances and cupboards. A design is agreed and a three-dimensional illustration of how the finished kitchen will look is printed out and given to the customer.

     (a) Name **one output device** that will be needed during the design stage of the kitchen planning. (1)

     (b) A very accurate and high-quality printout of the final design is needed for the installers to work from. Name **one** suitable **output device** that could produce this high-quality plan. (1)

     (c) Describe **two** advantages of producing kitchen designs in this way rather than drawing them by hand. (2)

Web tasks

1. Visit the Free On-Line Dictionary of Computing (FOLDOC) at:
    http://wombat.doc.ic.ac.uk/foldoc/

    (a) Look up definitions of the keywords highlighted in this chapter.

    (b) Prepare a summary list of keywords and definitions to use for revision.

2. Visit the PC Technology Guide at **www.pctechguide.com** to find out more about how **dot matrix**, **inkjet** and **laser printers** work.

    Use the information you find to prepare a fact sheet about these printers that would help an inexperienced computer user decide which type to buy.

ICT in supermarkets

Supermarkets use computer systems to:

- sell goods to customers and process payments at the checkouts;

- monitor and control stock by automatically generating orders for more products when the number in stock falls below a certain level;

- perform sales analysis to find out which products are selling well and which ones aren't;

- collect data about customers using loyalty cards, which offer points whenever money is spent in the store. This data is used to analyse the spending habits of customers and send them offers for the type of products that they buy regularly.

Electronic point of sale (EPOS) systems

Supermarket checkouts are called **electronic point of sale (EPOS) terminals**. You might also come across the term **electronic funds transfer point of sale (EFTPOS)** this simply refers to an EPOS terminal that can handle credit or debit card payments. Every EPOS terminal in a supermarket is connected to a minicomputer in the store, where a database of product information is stored. This computer is linked to the supermarket chain's mainframe computer using a telecommunications link such as a telephone line telephone line or satellite dish.

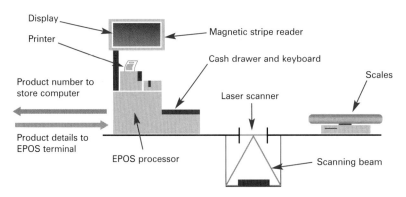

Figure CS1.1 The parts of a typical EPOS terminal

Barcodes

UK supermarkets use the **European Article Number** (or **EAN**) barcode system. This uses barcodes to represent a thirteen-digit **EAN number**, which identifies a product, its country of origin and manufacturer. The last digit of an EAN is a **check digit**, which is used to make sure the number has been input correctly (check digits will be explained further in Chapter 10).

The first 2 digits identify the country of manufacture

The next 5 digits identify the manufacturer

The last digit is the check digit

These 5 digits represent the product code

5 001935 014327

Figure CS1.2 The parts of an EAN product barcode

Online grocery shopping

One increasingly popular service offered by supermarkets is online shopping, which allows customers to order their groceries from home and have them delivered to their doors.

The main advantage offered by this type of service is that there's no need to visit the store, so people who work unsocial hours or find it difficult to leave the house can still do their shopping.

The main disadvantages of ordering groceries online are:

- you can't examine goods yourself before buying them;
- items that are out of stock could be replaced with something similar that you don't really want and may have to send back.

*Figure CS1.3 The home page of Tesco's online shopping service,
which was the first to be launched by a UK supermarket*

Stock control

Supermarkets use EPOS systems to monitor and control how much stock they hold. It is important that a supermarket has enough stock to make sure customers can buy the goods they need, but not too much of any one product so that it takes up a lot of space or ends up being thrown away once the sell-by date has passed.

When a product is sold, the following sequence of events takes place:

- a barcode scanner is used to read the EAN number from the product;
- the EAN number is sent by the EPOS terminal to the branch computer;
- the branch computer uses the EAN number to search the stock file for the product's price and description, which it sends back to the EPOS terminal;
- the branch computer updates the stock level for the product to show that one has been sold;
- the product's price and description are displayed at the EPOS terminal and printed on a receipt;
- the price of the product is added to the total of the products processed so far.

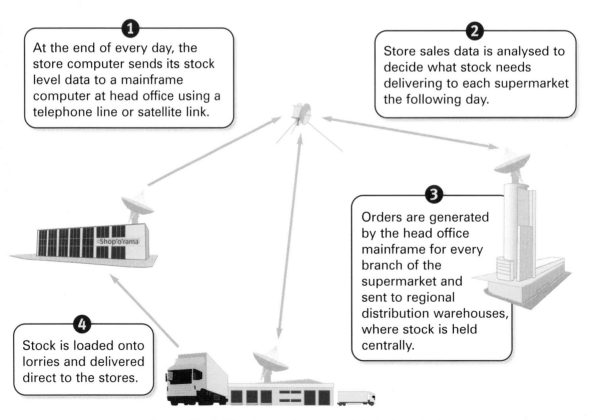

1 At the end of every day, the store computer sends its stock level data to a mainframe computer at head office using a telephone line or satellite link.

2 Store sales data is analysed to decide what stock needs delivering to each supermarket the following day.

3 Orders are generated by the head office mainframe for every branch of the supermarket and sent to regional distribution warehouses, where stock is held centrally.

4 Stock is loaded onto lorries and delivered direct to the stores.

Figure CS1.4 The stages of supermarket stock control

Figure CS1.5 One of a large supermarket chain's regional distribution centres

In the examination you could be asked to give (or choose from a list) some advantages or disadvantages of using EPOS systems in a supermarket.

Some of the advantages are:

- shelves are always well stocked, fresh food is readily available and products very rarely run out;
- customers can be dealt with much more quickly at the checkout;
- customers receive a fully itemised receipt;
- goods can be paid for at the till with a credit or debit card using electronic funds transfer (EFT);
- accurate and up-to-date sales analysis information is always available for managers;
- customer buying patterns can be analysed and used to target customers with offers for goods and services that they might be interested in.

Some of the disadvantages are:

- EPOS systems are expensive to install;
- EPOS systems require regular maintenance;
- technology must be kept up-to-date if a competitive edge is to be maintained against rival supermarkets' systems.

TIP

Questions

1.   (a) What do the letters **EPOS** stand for?   (1)

    (b) Draw and label a diagram of an EPOS terminal.   (6)

2.   (a) Describe **two input devices** used at an EPOS terminal   (2)

    (b) Give **two output devices** used at an EPOS terminal   (2)

    (c) Supermarket EPOS terminals are connected to the store computer.

        Explain why this is necessary.   (2)

    (d) Describe **one** other way that supermarkets use computers.   (2)

3. Supermarkets use **EPOS systems** to monitor and control stock levels.

    (a) Explain why it is necessary for a supermarket to monitor and control stock levels.   (2)

    (b) Describe the steps that take place from an individual product being sold through to more of that product being delivered to a store when stock levels become too low.   (5)

Web tasks

1. Visit the Free On-Line Dictionary of Computing (FOLDOC) at:
   http://wombat.doc.ic.ac.uk/foldoc/

   (a) Look up definitions of the keywords highlighted in this chapter.

   (b) Prepare a summary list of keywords and definitions to use
       for revision.

2. Find the online shopping web sites for at least **three** supermarket chains.

   Prepare a short presentation that describes for each site:

   - where to find the site;
   - the types of goods and services available;
   - the different ways you can find a particular product;
   - which site you think is the best and why;
   - which site you think is the worst and why.

An **operating system** is a set of programs that controls how the hardware of a computer works. An operating system provides a means of communication between the user and the computer, deals with the loading and running of application programs and manages the transfer of data and files to and from peripheral devices. The most widely used operating systems are called Microsoft Windows (e.g. Windows 2000, Window XP), MacOS (for Apple Mac computers), Novell Netware and UNIX. The operating system that a computer has also determines what application software will run on it. Application software will only work on a computer that has the operating system with which it was designed to be used.

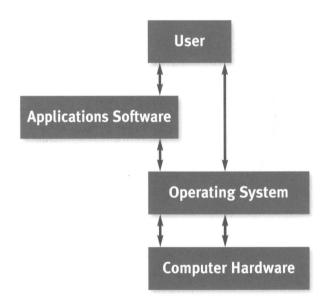

Figure 6.1 The operating system acts as a bridge between applications software and computer hardware. Users need application software to carry out the tasks that they require. The application software needs the operating system so that it can communicate with the hardware and get it to carry out hardware-related tasks such as printing or transferring data to and from backing storage devices. Application software and computer hardware cannot function without an operating system.

Functions of an operating system

An operating system carries out the following functions:

- It deals with input and output, which involves:
  - accepting data from input devices and transferring it to the computer's memory;
  - making sure that any output is sent to the correct output device.
- It manages the transfer of data between the computer's memory and backing storage devices.
- It manages system resources, which involves:
  - allocating memory space to programs and data;
  - keeping track of which parts of the memory have already been allocated and the parts that are still free.
- It deals with the loading of application software into memory and controls the execution, or 'running' of them. It also provides a way for applications software to communicate with the computer's hardware.
- It deals with any errors that occur when a program is being run, or when data is being transferred somewhere, and informs the user if necessary.
- It manages system security, which involves:
  - monitoring and restricting access to programs and data;
  - preventing unauthorised access to the system.
- It provides a **human computer interface**, or **HCI**, for the user (the different types of human computer interface that an operating system can provide are described in the next chapter).
- It provides special facilities for **multiprogramming**.

In the examination you could be asked to give, or choose from a list, some of the tasks carried out by operating systems. Some of the most important tasks based on the functions described above are:

- *start up the computer;*
- *manage memory space;*
- *manage the loading and running of programs;*
- *manage the loading, transfer and storage of data;*
- *manage system security.*

TIP

Multiprogramming operating systems

A multiprogramming operating system can hold more than one program in memory at the same time. There are two types of multiprogramming operating system; **multitasking** and **multiuser**.

A **multitasking** operating system allows two or more programs to run at the same time. The operating system does this by swapping each program in and out of memory in turn. When a program is swapped out of memory it is stored temporarily on disk until it is needed again. Windows 2000 is an example of a multitasking operating system.

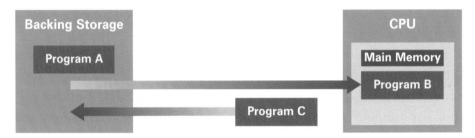

Figure 6.2 A multitasking operating system.

Program C is transferred out of main memory to backing storage as Program B is transferred back into memory. Program A is not needed yet and waits in backing storage

A **multiuser** operating system lets many users at different terminals share processing time on a powerful central computer. The operating system does this by switching rapidly between the terminals giving each one in turn a small amount of processor time on the central computer. The operating system switches so quickly between the terminals that each user appears to have uninterrupted access to the central computer. However, if there are a large number of users on such a system, the time that it takes the central computer to respond can become more noticeable.

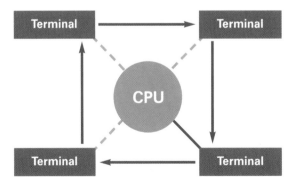

Figure 6.3 A multitasking operating system. Each terminal in turn gets a small amount of processor time called a 'time slice'. Only one terminal at a time has access to the CPU

Utility programs

Utility programs are usually supplied along with an operating system. They are used to carry out routine tasks that are often needed by a user. Some of the routine tasks performed by utility programs are:

- compressing a file to save space on backing storage;
- defragmenting a disk drive;
- recovering data from damaged file;
- checking a disk for faults and repairing them;
- formatting a floppy disk;
- checking the files on a disk for computer viruses.

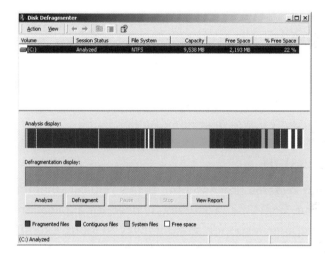

Figure 6.4 Defragmenting a hard disk drive with a Windows 2000 utility

Figure 6.5 Formatting a floppy disk with a Windows 2000 utility

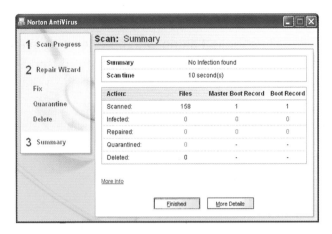

Figure 6.6 Using a virus-checking program.

Processing methods

A **processing method** is the way a particular operating system deals with input. There are three main types of processing method: **real-time**, **transaction** and **batch** processing. These processing methods, and some examples of applications that they would be used for, are described below.

Real-time processing

Real-time processing systems process input data so quickly that the resulting output can affect further input. Real-time processing is used for applications where it is essential that the computer responds straight away to input. Examples of applications where real-time processing is used are missile defence systems, automatic pilot systems on aircraft and monitoring intensive-care patients in a hospital.

The automatic pilot must use real-time processing so that it can respond instantly to any change in the aircraft's heading, speed or altitude

Figure 6.7 The flight deck of a Boeing 747 airliner

Transaction processing

Transaction processing (or **on-line processing**), is used for applications where input needs to be dealt with straight away, but it is not critical if there is a slight delay in the time that it takes for the computer to respond to requests. Examples of applications where transaction processing is used include the on-line seat booking systems used by airlines and the stock-control systems used by catalogue companies like Argos. A system where transaction processing is used will always give an up-to-the-minute picture of the current situation.

Batch processing

A **batch processing** system does not respond to input straight away. Instead, input is collected together into a '**batch**' while the system is **off-line**. When a batch is ready to be processed the system goes **on-line** to carry out the processing of the data. Batch processing is non-interactive. This means that the user cannot get an immediate response to input as they would with an interactive system. Examples of applications that use batch processing include producing gas, electricity or water bills and marking OMR sheets from multiple-choice examinations.

In the examination you could be asked to suggest the most suitable processing method for a variety of different applications.

Make sure you know and understand

* *the main differences between the processing methods described above;*
* *the kind of tasks they are used for.*

TIP

Questions

1.   (a) Explain what is meant by the term *operating system*.   (2)

(b) Operating systems are

	Tick **one** box only
Hardware	
Software	

(1)

(c)   Which **three** of the following are features of operating systems?

	Tick **three** box only
Manages system resources including memory	
Manages the allocation of CPU time	
Manages the spell-checker in a word processor	
Manages the accounts	
Manages system security	
Manages the buying of new computers	

(3)

(d) Name **two** different types of operating system.   (2)

AQA 2003 Higher Tier

2.   An operating system is a type of computer software.

(a) Give **four** tasks that are carried out by all operating systems.   (4)

(b Describe **one** additional task that a multi-tasking operating system would be able to carry out.   (2)

(c) Describe **one** additional task that a multi-user operating system would be able to carry out.   (2)

AQA (NEAB) 2002 Paper 2 Tier H

3.   (a)   What is a *utility program*?   (1)

(b)   Give **five** different types of task that utility programs perform.   (5)

4. For the applications listed below give a suitable type of processing method. In each case support your choice of processing method with at least **one** reason.

(a) Producing bills for a gas company

(b) Controlling the automatic pilot on an aircraft

(c) Processing cheques for a bank

(d) Theatre seat booking system

(e) Controlling a nuclear power station   (10)

Web tasks

1. Visit the free On-Line Dictionary of Computing (FOLDOC) at:
    http://wombat.doc.ic.ac.uk/foldoc/

    (a) Look up definitions of the keywords highlighted in this chapter.

    (b) Prepare a summary list of keywords and definitions to use
        for revision.

2. Visit **www.microsoft.com** and find the support pages for **Windows 2000** or
    Windows XP.

    Use the information you find there to write a simple set of instructions for an
    inexperienced computer user that describe how to do the following:

    *   format a floppy disk;

    *   defragment a hard disk drive.

    You could use other unofficial support sites to help with this task but check
    with your teacher first.

3. Find out more about the features offered by the most popular PC operating
    systems by visiting the sites of the companies that produce them. For **MacOS**
    visit **www.apple.com** and for **MS Windows** visit **www.microsoft.com**

The human–computer interface is what allows the user to communicate with the computer, and is often called simply the **user interface**. The three main types of user interface are **command-driven**, **menu-driven** and **graphical** (or **GUI**). These different types of user interface are described in this chapter.

Command-driven user interfaces

To use a command-driven system to communicate with the computer, the user has to type in special command words. DOS, which stands for Disk Operating System, is a very commonly used command-driven user interface.

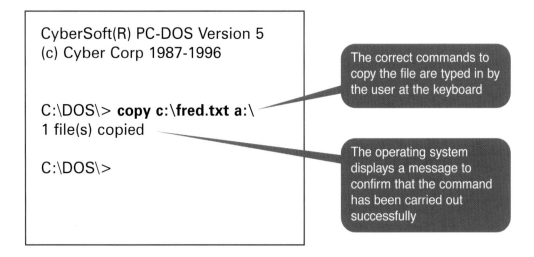

```
CyberSoft(R) PC-DOS Version 5
(c) Cyber Corp 1987-1996


C:\DOS\> copy c:\fred.txt a:\
1 file(s) copied

C:\DOS\>
```

The correct commands to copy the file are typed in by the user at the keyboard

The operating system displays a message to confirm that the command has been carried out successfully

Figure 7.1 Using a command-driven user interface to copy a file called fred.txt to the user's floppy disk

The main advantage of command-driven interfaces is that they can be quick to use as long as the user knows the correct commands. The main disadvantage of command-driven interfaces is that they are very difficult to use if the user is a beginner or doesn't know the correct commands. Command-driven systems can be very unfriendly and confusing for people who aren't computer experts.

Menu-driven user interfaces

Menu-driven systems offer the user lists of options which they can select by pressing a particular key on the keyboard. Most menu-driven systems have a 'main menu', which has options on it that offer the user other menu screens once they have been selected.

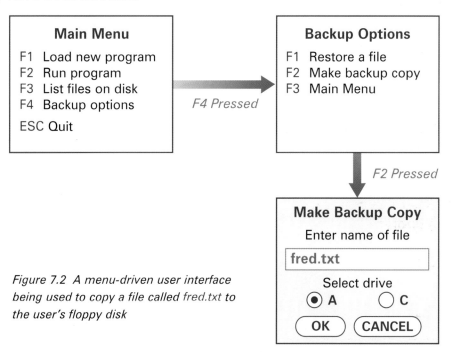

Figure 7.2 A menu-driven user interface being used to copy a file called fred.txt to the user's floppy disk

The main advantage of menu-driven systems is that they are easy to use. The user is taken step-by-step through a series of options until a particular task has been completed. The main disadvantage of menu-driven systems is that they can be quite 'long-winded'. Getting to one particular option can often involve going through two, three or even more different menu screens.

Graphical user interfaces

The most widely used type of **graphical user interfaces** are **WIMP** systems. WIMP stands for **W**indows **I**cons **M**enu **P**ointer. Options are represented by small pictures (or '**icons**') arranged inside rectangular boxes called **windows**. To choose an option represented by an icon, the user uses a mouse to move a pointer on the screen over the icon and then 'double-clicks' on it with the mouse button. To choose an item from a menu the user clicks on a word in the **menu bar**. This reveals a **drop-down menu** with a list of options. To choose an option the user points to it and clicks once on the mouse button.

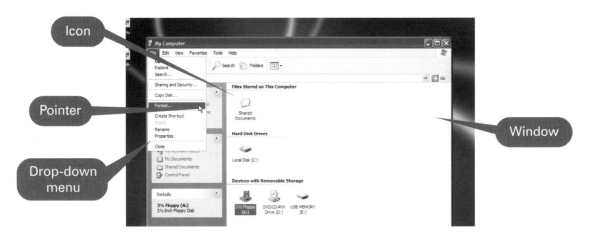

Figure 7.3 The MS Windows XP graphical user interface

The main advantage of graphical user interfaces is that they are very easy to use, especially for a beginner. The main disadvantage is the amount of memory space they need. A graphical user interface like Windows needs a lot of RAM to run properly. As well as using up a lot of RAM, graphical user interfaces also take up a large amount of hard disk space.

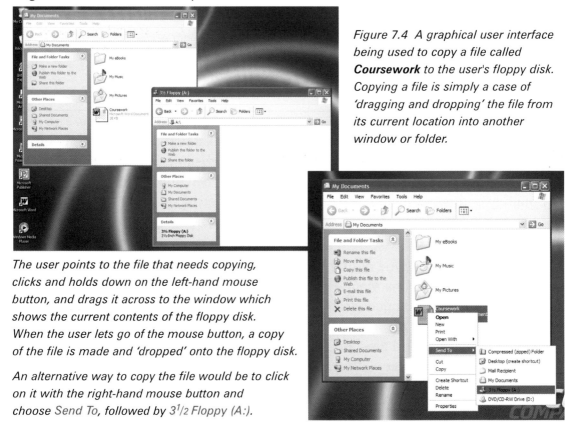

Figure 7.4 A graphical user interface being used to copy a file called **Coursework** to the user's floppy disk. Copying a file is simply a case of 'dragging and dropping' the file from its current location into another window or folder.

The user points to the file that needs copying, clicks and holds down on the left-hand mouse button, and drags it across to the window which shows the current contents of the floppy disk. When the user lets go of the mouse button, a copy of the file is made and 'dropped' onto the floppy disk.

An alternative way to copy the file would be to click on it with the right-hand mouse button and choose Send To, followed by $3^1/2$ Floppy (A:).

In the examination you could be asked to identify or list some different types of user interface. Make sure you can describe the main features and advantages of command-driven, menu-driven and graphical user interfaces.

User interface design

A good user interface should be **user-friendly**. This means that even inexperienced users should be able to learn quite quickly and easily how to use it. To make a user interface user-friendly, care must be taken when it is being designed. Some of the factors that should be considered when designing a new user interface are:

- The way that the different parts of the user interface are operated should be consistent. This is so that, when a user has learnt how to do one thing, it will be easier for them to learn how to do other things in a similar way.

- The layout of the screen and the positioning of items such as windows, icons and menus on the screen should be consistent.

- Colours should be chosen that are easy to see. For example, black text on a dark blue background is a poor combination. Also, colours should be chosen to be consistent with what people are used to: you would not use a green box for warning and a red box to mean 'OK — continue'.

- Sound can be used to do things such as alerting the user to problems, but it should also be possible to turn it off.

- On-line help is often a useful feature. This means that the user can call up help on the screen and not have to stop what they're doing to refer to a manual.

In the examination you could be asked to choose or describe some of the factors that should be taken into account when a new user interface is being designed. Make sure that you know and understand the points listed above.

Questions

1. Jane is a systems analyst. She has been asked to design a user interface for a bank's cashpoint machines.

   The pictures below show three different types of user interface.

C:\format a:\	Menu
	1. Format disk
	2. Disk directory
	3. Quit
	   Enter required
	   option number	

Interface 1	Interface 2	Interface 3

   (a) Name each of these types of user interface.

   Interface 1 .... (1)

   Interface 2 .... (1)

   Interface 3 .... (1)

   (b) Choose **five** factors from the list below that Jane should consider when she designs the user interface.

   Tick five boxes only

The contents of the online help facility	
The size of the cash machine	
The position of items on the screen	
How much a cash machine costs	
How to use colour	
How many people will use it	
Who will use the interface	
The sounds that will be needed	

   (5)

(c) (i) Which one of the user interfaces you named in part (a) would be the most suitable type for Jane to design for the bank's cashpoint machines? (1)

(ii) Give **two** reasons why the type of interface you have given in part (i) above would be the most suitable. (2)

AQA (NEAB) 2002 Paper 2 Tier F

2. The way in which a user interacts with computer software is important. A good Human Computer Interface makes software easy to use. Explain how the user makes choices in each of the following types of interface.

(a) A graphical user interface. (2)

(b) A menu-driven user interface. (2)

(c) A command-driven user interface. (1)

AQA (NEAB) 1999 Paper 2 Tier F

3. Graphical user interfaces (GUIs) are found on many computers.

(a) Why do computers need a user interface? (1)

(b) Give **one** input device, other than a keyboard, that can be used with a graphical user interface. (1)

(c) Give **four** features of a graphical user interface. (4)

(d) (i) Give **one** other type of user interface. (1)

(ii) Give **two** benefits to an inexperienced user offered by a graphical user interface compared to this type of interface. (2)

AQA (NEAB) 2001 Paper 2 Tier H

Web tasks

1. Visit the Free On-Line Dictionary of Computing (FOLDOC) at:
    http://wombat.doc.ic.ac.uk/foldoc/

    (a) Look up definitions of the keywords highlighted in this chapter.

    (b) Prepare a summary list of keywords and definitions to use for revision.

2. Find out more about the history and development of graphical user interfaces (GUIs) at **http://toastytech.com/guis/**

There are two main types of computer software: **system software** and **application software**. System software includes the operating system and utility programs, and has already been discussed. **Application software** carries out a particular type of task for a user. Word processors, spreadsheets, databases, programs to control robots or fly aeroplanes, to calculate a company payroll or keep track of how many cans of baked beans are left in a supermarket are all examples of application software. Application software can be classified as **general-purpose**, **specialist** or **tailor-made**.

General-purpose application packages

A **general-purpose application package** is a type of software that can perform many different related tasks. Word processors, spreadsheets, databases, graphics and presentation software are all examples of application packages. This type of software is sometimes called **generic** software. This means, for example, that any one of the many different word-processing packages that you could buy will do the same general sorts of tasks as the others. Most computer users buy application packages 'off-the-shelf'. There are several good reasons for using this type of ready-made software — some of these are:

- it is relatively cheap;
- it is readily available and can be installed quickly and easily;
- it will have been thoroughly tested so there will be very little chance of it having any serious faults or 'bugs';
- it will be well supported with a lot of books available about how to use it, as well as on-line help and discussions on the Internet.

The most common types of general purpose software, and the types of tasks that they can be used for, are listed below:

- **Database packages** (e.g. MS Access, FileMaker Pro, FoxPro) are used to store and retrieve information;
- **Spreadsheet packages** (e.g. MS Excel, Lotus 123) are used for tasks that involve a lot of calculations or for the production of graphs and charts;
- **Word processing packages** (e.g. MS Word, WordPerfect) are used to produce text-based documents such as letters, reports and memos;
- **Desktop publishing (DTP) packages** (e.g. MS Publisher, PageMaker, PagePlus) are used to produce professional-quality publications such as posters, books, newsletters, newspapers and magazines;

Chapter 8

- **Graphics packages** (e.g. Paint, PaintBrush, Serif Draw, Corel Draw) are used to produce and manipulate artwork;
- **Computer-aided design (CAD)** packages (e.g. 2D-Design, AutoCAD, TurboCAD) are used to produce engineering designs and architectural plans;
- **Communications software** (e.g. Internet Explorer, Netscape Communicator, MS Outlook) is used to access the Internet and send and receive e-mail;
- **Presentation graphics packages** (e.g. PowerPoint, Lotus Freelance) are used to create slide shows and presentations, which can be viewed on-screen or with a projector;
- **Web design packages** (e.g. MS FrontPage, Macromedia Dreamweaver) are used to create web pages.

  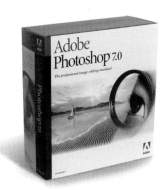

Figure 8.1 Some popular general-purpose application packages

TIP

In the examination you could be asked to give, or choose from a list, the most suitable type of application software for different tasks. Make sure you know and can describe the tasks for which each different type of application software listed above is used.

Integrated packages

An integrated package combines many different types of application together in one single package. This type of software normally offers facilities for word processing, spreadsheets, databases, graphics, presentation and communications.

The advantages of using integrated packages are:

- it is much cheaper to buy one integrated package than several separate application packages;

- different applications have the same user interface;

- data can be transferred quickly and easily between applications;

- they are much quicker to install than several separate application packages.

The main problem with integrated packages is that their individual applications have a limited number of features compared with equivalent single application packages. MS Works is an example of an integrated package. Integrated packages are not very common and have gradually been replaced by applications bundled together by software manufacturers and sold as suites of programs. These bundles offer the advantages of applications with a complete set of features, a common user interface and easy facilities for sharing and exchanging data.

Figure 8.2 Some popular program suites

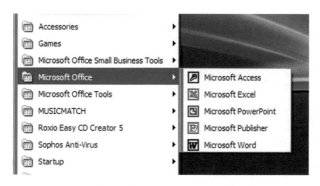

Figure 8.3

Microsoft Office 2000 is an example of a bundled suite of application programs — database, spreadsheet, word processing, presentation and desktop publishing software are included

Specialist application software

Specialist application software performs a single very specific type of task. Programs to work out payroll, calculate accounts, plan driving routes, work out income tax returns, deal with stock control and handle appointments are all examples of specialist application software.

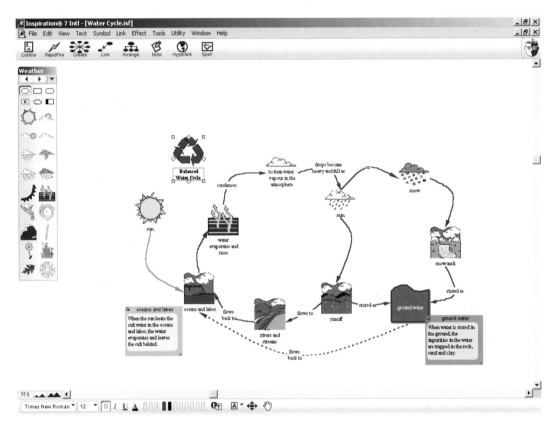

Figure 8.4

Mind-mapping software is an example of specialist application software

Tailor-made software

Sometimes an organisation finds that 'off-the-shelf' software will not do exactly what it wants. In this case they might decide to have special tailor-made (or **bespoke**) software specially developed for the purpose. The main drawbacks of this approach are the high cost and the long time that some programs take to develop.

Buying new software

Application software can be very expensive — especially for a large business that may need many copies or special licences to be able to use the software on all their computers. Choosing the wrong software can be a very costly mistake. There are a number of questions (or **"evaluation criteria"**) that should be considered before the final choice is made. Some of the most important questions are:

- What sort of tasks will the software be used for?
- How much does the software cost and how much money is available to buy it?
- What operating system does the software need? Software will only work with the operating system that it was designed for.

- What are the minimum system requirements for the software? Every application package has a minimum set of hardware requirements, such as how much hard disk space and memory are needed.
- Will the software be used on a single computer or on a network? If the software is going to be used on a network, a special version of it may be needed.
- How much support is available for users? This could be in the form of on-line help, telephone support lines, websites and printed manuals. More popular software will have more of these resources.
- How easy is the software to install — can an ordinary user carry out the installation or will an ICT expert be needed to do it?

Questions

1. From the list below, choose the **most** suitable type of application software to use for each task described.

Charts	Drawing
Communications	Mail-merging
Database	Spreadsheet
Data logging	Web design
Desk top publishing	Word processing

   Task

   (a) sending an e-mail

   (b) sending a personalised letter to all members of a club

   (c) writing a book

   (d) calculating the monthly cost of running a car

   (e) automatically collecting temperatures at a weather station

   (f) storing a video club's membership records

   (g) organising the layout of a school newspaper   (7)

   AQA 2003 Higher Tier

2. The owner of a riding stables with 25 horses wants to use a computer system to carry out the following tasks:-

   Task1   Produce a price list to give to the customers.

   Task 2   Send special offer advertisements to all customers.

   Task 3   Store the upkeep costs such as feed and vet's bills for each horse.

   Task 4   Keep a record of bookings for all the horses.

   To carry out these tasks the owner could buy an integrated package or buy separate software packages.

   (a) Give **two** advantages of buying an integrated package.   (2)

   (b) Give **two** advantages of buying separate software packages.   (2)

   AQA (NEAB) 2001 Paper 1 Tier H

3. Computers need both **system software** and **applications software**.

    (a) Explain why computers need both types of software. (2)

    (b) Give **three** different categories of application software. (3)

    (c) Explain what is meant by the term **application package**. (2)

    (d) Describe briefly **five** evaluation criteria that could be used by a user when choosing a new application package for their PC. (5)

4. Jean Davies owns two high street shops that sell fashion clothes and accessories aimed at teenagers. Her company already has a computer system that is used for word processing but she wants to buy software that will help her with stock control. She must decide whether to buy an existing software package or have one specially written for her company.

    (a) Give **two** advantages to her of buying an existing software package. (2)

    (b) Give **two** advantages to her of having a piece of software specially written. (2)

    (c) Whichever of these two she eventually buys, the software will come complete with user documentation.
State **four** sections which the user documentation would normally contain. (4)

AQA (NEAB) 2000 Paper 1 Tier F

5. Explain why commercial applications packages are not always exactly suited to the needs of a business user and describe how these limitations can be overcome. (5)

Web tasks

1. Visit the Free On-Line Dictionary of Computing (FOLDOC) at:
    http://wombat.doc.ic.ac.uk/foldoc/

    (a) Look up definitions of the keywords highlighted in this chapter.

    (b) Prepare a summary list of keywords and definitions to use for revision.

2. Visit **www.egghead.com** and **www.computerworld.com**

    (a) Find articles about the general purpose application packages you use at school or home.

    (b) Use the information you find to write about the system requirements and strengths and weaknesses of these packages (this will be useful for your coursework).

3. Visit **www.shareware.com** and **www.shareware.org**

    (a) Find out what the terms **shareware** and **freeware** mean.

    (b) Prepare a summary that describes the advantages and disadvantages of using these types of software

Manual filing systems

Computers have been used to store information since the middle of the last century. Before we had computers, information was stored on pieces of paper or card in **manual filing systems**. A manual filing system means something like a **filing cabinet** or **card index**.

In Figure 9.1 a school is storing information about its students on record cards. These cards are stored in alphabetical order in a box. This is an example of a card-index filing system. Each student has their own card; this is their **record**. On a student's card, certain things about the student (like name and date of birth) are recorded; these individual pieces of information are called **fields**.

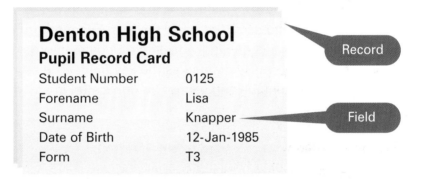

Figure 9.1 Records in a manual card-index filing system

There are many problems with storing information manually, and it was partly because of these problems that computers were invented. The problems associated with manual filing systems are:

- Searching through all of the records to find answers to questions about the information can be very time-consuming. Suppose a health centre kept all of its patient's medical records in filing cabinets, and needed a list of all the women who had given birth in the last six months. To get this list, someone would have to search through all of the female patients' medical records by hand and look for everyone who had given birth in the last six months. This would be very time-consuming and there would be no guarantee that some records would not get overlooked.

- Large manual filing systems take up a lot of space. This can be expensive for businesses and other organisations because they need more office space, which they have to rent or buy. It also costs more to light and heat a larger office.

- Paper-based records are easily damaged or mixed up with other papers and lost.

• Records are often put back in the wrong place. This makes it much harder to find them next time they're needed.

Computer-based filing systems

Computers are used to store information because they solve all of these problems. A computer-based filing system can store a lot of information in a very small space, search through the information very quickly and produce printed lists and reports very easily.

Data files

Information in computer-based filing systems is stored in **data files**. A file is a collection of related **records**: this means that each record in a file contains the same sort of information as all the other records. Every record must have at least one **field** – a field contains one individual item of data. In order to identify individual records, one field is normally defined as the **key field**. The key field in each record of a data file must be unique and cannot be duplicated in any other record.

> These are the **fields** – there are **four** fields in each record of this file.
>
> ISBN is the **key field**. This is the field that has a different value in every record. It is used to distinguish one record from another. Some books could have the same title, author or publisher. The ISBN is the only way a particular book can be picked out.
>
> **A key field uniquely identifies an individual record.**

ISBN	Title	Author	Publisher
1-23761-121-3	Complete Cat Care	Claudia Heiniken	Stones and Douglas
1-37463-126-4	Build Your Own Boat	Brian Deacon	Taylor & Co
1-26834-217-7	Better Homes	Julia Stone	Taylor & Co
1-86272-341-5	Practical Pottery	Dennis Cooper	NTC International
1-32627-219-3	DIY Welding	Jane Masters	Stones and Douglas

> This is one completed record – there are five records in this file.

Figure 9.2 Part of a data file used by a bookshop to store information about the books they sell. The records are related because each one stores information about a book for sale in the shop

*In the examination you could be asked to explain the basic terms associated with data files. Make sure you know, and can explain with examples, the meaning of the terms: **file, record, field** and **key field**.*

Fixed and variable length records

A **fixed length record** is one where the length of the fields in each record has been set to be a certain maximum number of characters long. Suppose a field that was going to contain a name was set to be 25 characters long: this means that the field could only ever contain up to 25 characters. If all of the fields in the record have a fixed length like this then the record is said to be a fixed length record. The problem with fixed length records is that each field very rarely contains the maximum number of characters allowed, which means that a lot of space is needlessly set aside and wasted. Also, values sometimes cannot be entered because they are too large to fit in the space allowed in a field.

The advantage of fixed length records is that they make file processing much easier because the start and end of each record is always a fixed number of characters apart. This makes it much easier to locate both individual records and fields.

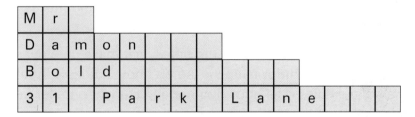

Figure 9.3 Fixed length records

A set amount of storage space is set aside for each field. If the contents of a field don't fill the space completely some of it remains empty and is wasted

A **variable length record** is one where the length of a field can change to allow data of any size to fit. The advantage of variable length records is that space is not wasted – only the space needed is ever used. The main problem with variable length records is that it is much more difficult to locate the start and end of individual records and fields. This is because they are not separated by a fixed number of characters. To separate variable length records, each field has a special character to mark where it ends – called an **end-of-field marker**. When records need to be located the computer must count through the end-of-field markers to locate individual records and fields.

M	r	#	D	a	m	o	n	#	B	o	l	d	#
3	1		P	a	r	k		L	a	n	e	#	

Figure 9.4 Variable length records

A special marker (# in this example) indicates where each field ends. The length of a field depends upon the data that is placed in it. Only the space needed for a field is ever used – so none is wasted

Relational databases

A **database** is a structured collection of related data. It can be a single file that contains a large number of records, or a collection of files. Many modern databases are described as being **relational**. This just describes the way that data is organised within the database.

A relational database consists of one or more **tables**, which contain information about **entities**. An entity is simply one type of object or 'thing', such as a student in a school, a book in a library or a product for sale in a shop. The information about each individual entity makes up one **record**, which is divided up into **fields** just as in an ordinary data file. A field contains one individual item of data about an entity – such as the name of a student.

Each type of entity is stored in a separate table. Tables are linked together by common fields. The links between tables are called **relationships**. Setting up relationships between tables avoids the duplication of data and makes it much easier to update the information in the database.

The example shown in Figure 9.5 shows the tables that make up a relational database for a school library. Information is stored about students, books and loans – these are the entities. The book number and student number fields are used to link the tables together. So, for example, even though a loan record does not contain the title of a book on loan, this can be "looked up" in the books table using the book number.

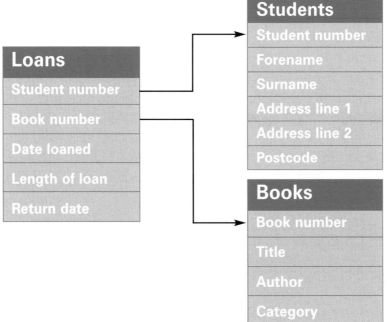

Figure 9.5 Linked data tables in the relational database for a school library

A relational database is made up from a number of different parts (or **objects**). The first stage in setting up a new relational database is to produce a design that describes the objects needed in the database. The main object types that should be considered when preparing this design are:

Tables

The database designer must think carefully about exactly what information needs to be stored about each entity and specify the tables and fields that will be needed. For each field the **data type** and any **validation check** (these are explained in the next chapter) must be specified at this stage.

Queries

Searching (or **interrogating**) a database involves looking for an individual record or group of records that matches a certain condition. To start a search the user must enter a **search command** (or **query**). This tells the database software which fields to look at in each record and what to look for. The results of a query can be displayed on screen or printed out as a list or report. The database designer must decide what queries are needed. For each query, the designer must say what information to look for, which tables to use and which fields to display.

Forms

On-screen forms are used to view and change information. Well-designed forms allow information to be entered or changed quickly and easily, and help to reduce errors when data is being entered. The database designer must decide which forms are needed. For each form, the designer must state which tables it will use, choose the fields that will be displayed and think carefully about the layout.

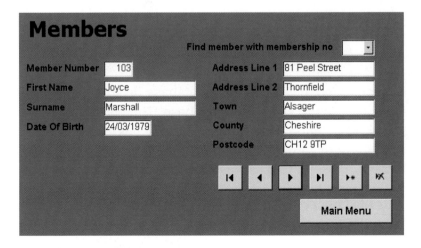

Figure 9.6 This on-screen form is part of an MS Access database

Reports

Reports are used to summarise and print out information. Reports are often used to display the information found by a query. The database designer must decide which reports are needed. For each report the designer must state which tables or queries it will use, choose the fields that will be displayed and think carefully about the layout.

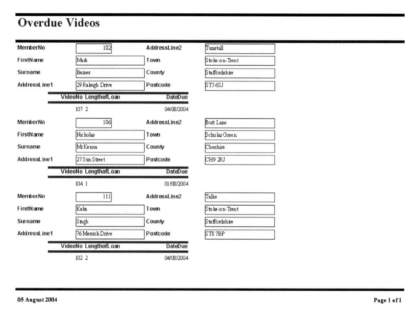

Figure 9.7 *This report is part of an MS Access database*

File operations

File operations are the different things that can be done to a computer file. The main types of file operation are **searching**, **sorting**, **merging** and **updating**.

Searching

We have already mentioned that preparing a database design involves specifying the queries that will be used to search the database. The way that a query searches a database depends on both the type of query and the **search criteria** entered by the user. Some of the more common types of query are described below.

Equals

This type of query will find all the records where the data in a field is **equal to** a certain value. The symbol = is often used to represent the words EQUAL TO or EQUALS in this type of query. Some software packages do use the words EQUAL

TO or EQUALS, or an abbreviation such as EQ, instead of a symbol. Exactly what you need to type will depend upon the database package you are using.

Part of an estate agent's property database is shown in the table below.

Property	Type	Street	Town	Postcode	Beds	Baths	Garage	Price
1200	TER	21 Lowther Street	Canford	CN21 9XJ	2	1	N	£119,995
1201	SEM	74 Grange Road	Canford	CN17 2BF	3	1	S	£144,995
1202	SEM	69 Fairfield Street	Canford	CN20 8HQ	4	2	S	£160,000
1203	BUN	14 Taybor Avenue	Gorton	GR11 3JB	4	2	D	£175,495
1204	DET	181 High Lane	Canford	CN17 8JU	5	2	D	£199,995
1205	TER	42 Cornwall Street	Canford	CN27 1BQ	2	1	N	£132,495
1206	DET	28 Horton Drive	Gorton	GR15 9FX	4	2	D	£179,995
1207	SEM	78 Grange Road	Canford	CN17 2BF	3	1	S	£143,495
1208	FLT	1219 Cresta Court	Gorton	GR9 11PK	2	1	N	£109,495
1209	BUN	27 Braymar Avenue	Canford	CN22 6CT	3	1	D	£154,995
1210	DET	45 Sherwood Road	Canford	CN26 9TY	4	2	D	£174,995
1211	TER	17 Skaymar Court	Gorton	GR12 6GP	3	1	N	£125,000

Suppose the estate agent wanted to search the database to find all the terraced houses for sale. They might use a query something like this:

List Street, Town, Beds, Price **For** Type **Equals** "TER"

This query would produce the result:

Street	Town	Beds	Price
21 Lowther Street	Canford	2	£119,995
42 Cornwall Street	Canford	2	£132,495
17 Skaymar Court	Gorton	3	£125,000

Field:	Street	Town	Beds	Price	Type
Table:	Properties	Properties	Properties	Properties	Properties
Sort:					
Show:	☑	☑	☑	☑	☐
Criteria:					"ter"
or:					

Figure 9.8 Setting up an equals query in MS Access

Greater than

This type of query will find all the records where the data in a field is **greater than** a certain value. The symbol > is often used to represent the words GREATER THAN in this type of query. Some software packages will use the words GREATER THAN or an abbreviation such as GT instead of a symbol. Exactly what you need to type will depend upon the database package you are using.

Suppose the estate agent wanted to search the database to find all the houses for sale over a particular price. They might use a query something like this:

List Street, Town, Price **For** Price **Greater than** 179995

This query would produce the result:

Street	Town	Price
181 High Lane	Canford	£199,995

Field:	Street	Town	Price
Table:	Properties	Properties	Properties
Sort:			
Show:	✔	✔	✔
Criteria:			>179995
or:			

Figure 9.9 Setting up a greater than query in MS Access

A slightly different version of this type of query will find all the records where the data in a field is **greater than or equal to** a certain value. The symbol >= is often used in this type of query to represent the words GREATER THAN OR EQUAL TO.

Suppose the estate agent wanted to search the database to find all the houses for sale equal to or over a particular price. They might use a query something like this:

List Street, Town, Price **For Price Greater than equal to** 179995

This query would produce the result:

Street	Town	Price
181 High Lane	Canford	£199,995
28 Horton Drive	Gorton	£179,995

Field:	Street	Town	Price
Table:	Properties	Properties	Properties
Sort:			
Show:	✔	✔	✔
Criteria:			>=179995
or:			

Figure 9.10 Setting up a greater than or equal to query in MS Access

Less than

This type of query will find all the records where the data in a field is **less than** a certain value. The symbol < is often used in this type of query to represent the words LESS THAN. Some software packages will use the words LESS THAN or an abbreviation such as LT instead of a symbol. Exactly what you need to type will depend upon the database package you are using.

Suppose the estate agent wanted to search the database to find all the houses for sale under a particular price. They might use a query something like this:

List Street, Town, Price **For** Price **Less than** 125000

This query would produce the result:

Street	Town	Price
21 Lowther Street	Canford	£119,995
1219 Cresta Court	Gorton	£109,495

Field:	Street	Town	Price
Table:	Properties	Properties	Properties
Sort:			
Show:	☑	☑	☑
Criteria:			<125000
or:			

Figure 9.11 Setting up a less than query in MS Access

A slightly different version of this type of query will find all the records where the data in a field is **less than or equal to** a certain value. The symbol <= is often used in this type of query to represent the words LESS THAN OR EQUAL TO.

Suppose the estate agent wanted to search the database to find all the houses for sale equal to or under a particular price. They might use a query something like this:

List Street, Town, Price **For** Price **Less than or equal to** 125000

This query would produce the result:

Street	Town	Price
21 Lowther Street	Canford	£119,995
1219 Cresta Court	Gorton	£109,495
17 Skaymar Court	Gorton	£125,000

Field:	Street	Town	Price
Table:	Properties	Properties	Properties
Sort:			
Show:	☑	☑	☑
Criteria:			<=125000
or:			

Figure 9.12 Setting up a less than or equal to query in MS Access

AND

This type of query will find all the records that match two or more search criteria. Most software packages use the word AND. Exactly what you need to type will depend upon the database package you are using.

Suppose the estate agent wanted to search the database to find all the semi-detached houses for sale under a particular price. They might use a query something like this:

List Street, Town, Price **For** Type **Equals** "SEM"

AND Price Less than 160000

This query would produce the result:

Street	Town	Price
74 Grange Road	Canford	£144,995
78 Grange Road	Canford	£143,495

Field:	Street	Town	Price	Type
Table:	Properties	Properties	Properties	Properties
Sort:				
Show:	☑	☑	☑	☐
Criteria:			<=160000	"sem"
or:				

Figure 9.13 Setting up an AND query in MS Access

This type of query can also be used to find all the records where the data in one or more fields lies within a range of values.

Suppose the estate agent wanted to search the database to find all houses for sale in a particular price range. They might use a query something like this:

List Street, Town, Price **For** Price **Greater than** 125000

AND Price **Less than** 150000

This query would produce the result:

Street	Town	Price
74 Grange Road	Canford	£144,995
42 Cornwall Street	Canford	£132,495
78 Grange Road	Canford	£143,495

Field:	Street	Town	Price
Table:	Properties	Properties	Properties
Sort:			
Show:	☑	☑	☑
Criteria:			>125000 And <160000
or:			

Figure 9.14 Setting up an AND query to find values in a range in MS Access

OR

This type of query will find all the records that match a choice of two or more search criteria. This type of search finds records that match any of the given search criteria. Most software packages use the word OR. Exactly what you need to type will depend upon the database package you are using.

Suppose the estate agent wanted to search the database to find all the houses for sale with either a certain number of bedrooms or a certain number of bathrooms. They might use a query something like this:

List Street, Beds, Baths **For** Beds **Equals** 3

OR Baths **Equals** 2

This query would produce the result:

Street	Beds	Baths
74 Grange Road	3	1
69 Fairfield Street	4	2
14 Taybor Avenue	4	2
181 High Lane	5	2
28 Horton Drive	4	2
78 Grange Road	3	1
27 Braymar Avenue	3	1
45 Sherwood Road	4	2
17 Skaymar Court	3	1

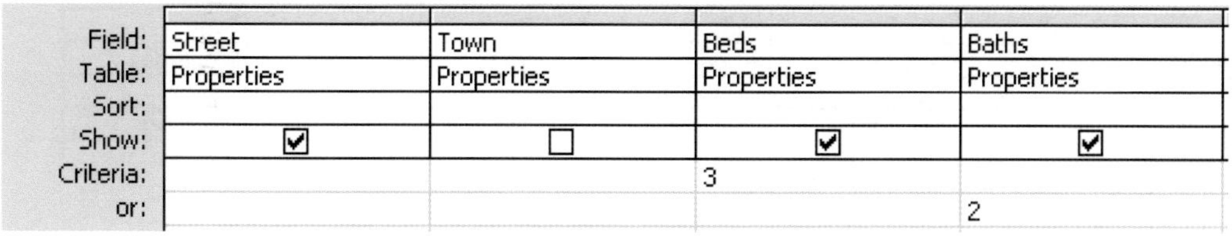

Field:	Street	Town	Beds	Baths
Table:	Properties	Properties	Properties	Properties
Sort:				
Show:	☑	☐	☑	☑
Criteria:			3	
or:				2

Figure 9.15 Setting up an OR query in MS Access

NOT

This type of query will find all the records that do not have a particular value in a field. The <> symbol is often used to represent the word NOT in this type of query. Some software packages may use the words NOT or NOT EQUAL instead of a symbol. Exactly what you need to type will depend upon the database package that you are using.

Suppose the estate agent wanted to search the database to find all the houses for sale that were not a certain type like semi-detached. They might use a query something like this:

List Street, Town, Price, Type **For** Type **Not equal** "SEM"

This query would produce the result:

Street	Town	Price	Type
21 Lowther Street	Canford	£119,995	TER
14 Taybor Avenue	Gorton	£175,495	BUN
181 High Lane	Canford	£199,995	DET
42 Cornwall Street	Canford	£132,495	TER
28 Horton Drive	Gorton	£179,995	DET
1219 Cresta Court	Gorton	£109,495	FLT
27 Braymar Avenue	Canford	£154,995	BUN
45 Sherwood Road	Canford	£174,995	DET
17 Skaymar Court	Gorton	£125,000	TER

Field:	Street	Town	Beds	Baths	Price	Type
Table:	Properties	Properties	Properties	Properties	Properties	Properties
Sort:						
Show:	☑	☑	☐	☐	☑	☑
Criteria:						<>"sem"
or:						

Figure 9.16 Setting up a NOT query in MS Access

TIP

In the examination you could be asked to give the results that you would get from using some sample search commands on part of a database file. You might also be asked to give the instructions that would be needed to find records matching certain conditions.

Make sure you know and understand the main differences between the different types of query or search commands described above.

The search commands you are likely to be asked to use in an examination question are:

List • For • Equals • Greater than • Less than • And • Or

It would also be good practice for you to carry out the example searches described above for the estate agent's database. You can use the MS Access query screenshots to help with this. The estate agent's database is available as an MS Access file in the student resources section of the publisher's website.

Sorting

Sorting involves putting the records in a file into a particular order, such as alphabetical order. In a student file, for example, a list of all the students in a particular form might need to be printed out in alphabetical order of student name.

Merging

Merging involves combining two files to produce one new file. This can be done by merging a file of new records to be added with another file that contains all of the existing records – called the **master file**.

Updating

The information stored in computer files must be kept up-to-date or it will cause problems for the business or organisation that is using it. Keeping the information in a file up-to-date involves adding new records when they're needed, deleting records that aren't needed and altering the information in a record when it changes. Suppose a mail order company wanted to send out a new catalogue to all its customers. If its customer records file wasn't up-to-date, catalogues could be sent to the wrong addresses. This would cost the company a lot of money in lost catalogues and business. To keep a file up-to-date it must be regularly updated. This involves **inserting**, **deleting** and **amending** records.

When a new record needs to be added to a file, it is **inserted**. In the estate agents database, for example, a new record would need to be inserted when a property came onto the market.

Records are **deleted** when they are no longer needed. In the estate agents database, for example, a record would need to be deleted when a property had been sold or taken off the market.

Records are **amended**, or changed, when the data in one or more of the fields needs to be altered for some reason. In the estate agents database, for example, a record would need to be amended if the price of a house was reduced.

Details of all the changes that need to be made to a master file are often collected together in a **transaction file**. The master file is updated by comparing it with the transaction file and making changes to any records that appear in both files. Normally at least three 'generations' of a master file are kept for backup purposes. If the latest version of the master file is damaged, it can be recreated by re-running the previous update using the old master and transaction files. This method of updating is known as the **grandfather-father-son** method.

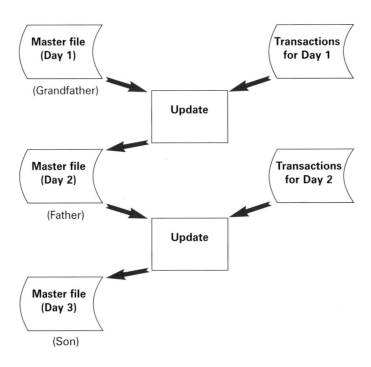

Figure 9.17 The grandfather-father-son method of updating

Backing up online databases

An on-line database is constantly being updated. To make sure no data is lost in the event of hardware failure, special back-up methods are used. **Transaction logging** and **RAID (Redundant Array of Inexpensive Disks)** are two commonly used methods.

Transaction logging involves storing the details of each update in a **transaction log file**. A 'before' and 'after' image of each updated record is also saved. If any part of the database is destroyed, an up-to-date copy can be recreated by a utility program using the transaction log file and the 'before' and 'after' images of the updated records.

RAID involves keeping several copies of a database on different disks at the same time. Whenever a record is updated, the same changes are made to each copy of the database. This is so that if one disk fails the data will still be safe on the others.

Database packages

Most databases are set-up using a **database package**. This is a piece of general-purpose application software which allows databases to be created and customised to meet a user's exact requirements. Some of the more popular database packages are MS Access, FileMaker Pro and FoxPro.

A typical database package will allow users to:

• create a file or table by entering their own field definitions;

• link tables together using common fields to create a relational database;

• specify automatic validation checks for fields (this is explained in the next chapter);

• add new fields to records or delete fields that are no longer needed;

• add, edit and delete records;

• perform simple and complex queries;

• import data from other applications;

• export data in standard file formats to other applications;

• create customised report forms for output;

• create customised data entry screens;

• create and link customised menu screens.

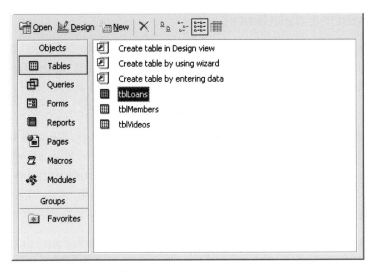

Figure 9.18 MS Access: a popular database package

In the examination you could be asked to give some of the advantages and disadvantages of using database packages.

Some of the advantages of using database packages are:

- large amounts of information can be stored in a very small space;
- information can be searched quickly;
- information can be updated easily;
- information can be presented in a variety of ways using graphs and reports;
- e-mail can be used to transfer information anywhere in the world instantly;
- new jobs are created because people are needed to write the software packages, build the hardware and train people.

TIP

Some of the disadvantages of using database packages are:

- the correct hardware and software need to be bought;
- people need to be trained to use the software;
- people who don't have the correct hardware and software won't be able to use the information;
- information can be lost or damaged due to human error, hacking or hardware failure;
- information can be altered without leaving any trace that changes have been made;
- businesses with computer-based information systems will need fewer employees than those with manual filing systems, which could lead to unemployment.

Questions

1. The table below shows part of a computer file used by a music shop to store information about its stock.

Title	Artist	Fomat	Status
Unhinged Melody	Roy & Jeremy	CD Single	In stock
Bounce	Nightshade	CD Album	Out of stock
Unhinged Melody	Terrance Tone	CD Single	In stock
Easy Street	The Vagabonds	CD Single	In stock
A Whiter Shade of Grey	Cliff Pilchard	CD Single	Out of stock
Greatest Hits III	David O'Connell	CD Album	In stock

    (a) How many **records** are shown in the table? (1)

    (b) How many **fields** are there in each record? (1)

    (c) What **data** is stored in the **third field** of the **fifth record**? (1)

    (d) What **data** is stored in the **first field** of the **second record**? (1)

    (e) Suggest a new field that could be added to each record and used as the **key field**. (1)

2. A ladies' fashion catalogue uses a database for stock control.

Part of the stock database is shown below.

Catalogue No	Size	Colour	Pattern	Price
1000345	12	Pink	Floral	27.99
1000347	12	Pink	Plain	29.50
1000429	14	Pink	Plain	29.50
1000438	16	Pink	Plain	39.99
1000513	14	Pink	Plain	34.99
1000516	14	Pink	Plain	41.75

    (a) Which field would be the best to use as the **key field**? (1)

    (b) Suggest **two** other fields that would need to be included in each stock record before the database file can be used for **stock control**. (2)

    (c) Explain briefly how these two fields can be used to maintain stock levels in the catalogue company's warehouse. (3)

3. A garage specialises in selling second-hand cars. A database is used to store information about the cars for sale. Part of the database file is shown below.

Make	Model	Colour	Number of doors	Registration number	Price	Additional feature
Audi	A4	Green	5	S772 FGS	£7249	Alloys
BMW	318 SE	Blue	4	M223 BMW	£4995	Full service history
BMW	520 SE	Green	4	TI25 GHB	£12495	Full electric pack
Citroen	Saxo	White	3	S132 HNM	£2450	Full service history
Fiat	Punto SX	Red	3	P56 TVB	£2195	Electric windows
Ford	Focus Zetec	Blue	5	Y579 PLM	£6995	Air conditioning
Ford	Mondeo	Blue	5	M673 FRD	£985	Full service history
Ford	Scorpio Ghia	Black	4	R778 THY	£5999	Metallic paint
Honda	Accord LS	Silver	4	S454 SAN	£6999	Full electric pack
Honda	Civic	White	3	S349 JNF	£2499	Power assisted steering
Nissan	Micra	Red	3	W789 PTE	£3999	Very low mileage
Peugeot	306 GTi	Yellow	3	P458 RTE	£4785	One owner
Renault	Laguna	Silver	5	SI10 BHW	£3999	Alloys
Rover	218S	Grey	5	M12 GHR	£999	Power assisted steering
Rover	420	Red	4	P134 HYT	£2999	Diesel
Rover	620 SLi	Green	4	R230 DDE	£3295	Full service history
Vauxhall	Astra Estate	Red	5	V94I XDS	£5499	One owner
Vauxhall	Sintra	Blue	7	T652 NBF	£6999	One owner
Volkswagen	Sharan	Green	7	P992 HGT	£4999	Low mileage
Volkswagen	Polo I.4E	Green	5	TJ51 TRE	£7999	Factory sun roof

(a) Explain what is meant by the following terms. You may find it helpful to give examples.

    (i) Record

    (ii) Field   (2)

(b) (i) Which field is the *key field* in this database?   (1)

    (ii) Explain why the field you have chosen is suitable to be used as a key field.   (1)

(c) In order to search the database, the following commands are used.

List
For
Equals
Greater than
Less than
And
Or

So the search
List Model **For** Colour **Equals** Silver

would produce the result
Accord LS
Laguna

What would be the results of the following searches?

(i) **List** Make **For** Number of doors **Equals** 7   (2)

(ii) **List** Model, Registration number **For** Price **Less than** £2000   (2)

(d) Write down the instructions needed to produce the following.

(i) A list of the model of cars that have a full service history as an additional feature.   (2)

(ii) A list of the make and model of cars, where the price of the car is between £3000 and £5000.   (3)

AQA 2003 Higher Tier

Web tasks

1. Visit the Free On-Line Dictionary of Computing (FOLDOC) at:

   http://wombat.doc.ic.ac.uk/foldoc/

   (a) Look up definitions of the keywords highlighted in this chapter.

   (b) Prepare a summary list of keywords and definitions to use for revision.

2. Relational databases often form just one part of much larger information systems.

   Visit **www.computerweekly.com/Article121440.htm**

   Prepare a one page summary of how the introduction of a new computer system has helped the coal authority to deal more efficiently with enquiries from house buyers.

3. Visit the websites of the software manufacturers listed below to find out more about their database products.

   Microsoft Access at:

   www.microsoft.com/office/access/prodinfo/overview.mspx

   Oracle Database 10g at:

   www.oracle.com/database/index.html?db_collateral.html

   IBM DB2 at:

   www-306.ibm.com/software/data/db2/udb/features.html

Collecting data

Much of the information stored in computer databases is collected using **data capture forms**. Examples of situations where a data capture form might be used include:

- application forms, e.g. for gym membership or to join a video rental shop;

- survey forms, e.g. census forms, consumer surveys, customer satisfaction questionnaires;

- product registration forms, e.g. product guarantees;

Data capture forms must be well designed so that they are easy to complete and collect all the required data for a record. A badly designed form could result in database records that contain incomplete or inaccurate data.

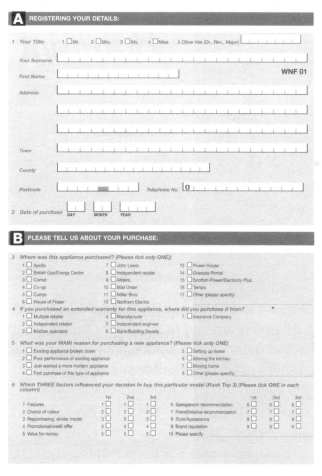

Figure 10.1 Part of the data capture form for a product guarantee. This is used to collect data about customers and the products they have purchased, which will be entered as a new record in a customer database

In the examination you could be asked to design a data capture form for a database.

In your answer to this type of question make sure that:

- *the field names you have included are clear and easy to read;*
- *you have used just boxes* ☐ *unless the question states that memo fields are required – for memo fields use lines like this*

_____

_____

- *don't fill in the form with examples unless the question says that you should;*
- *there are enough boxes next to each field name for data to be written down without running out of space – there are some suggestions in the examples below for the layout and minimum number of boxes to use for some common types of field;*

Field	Number
Title	3
First name	10
Surname	10
Street	10
Town	10
Postcode	7
Date of birth	8
Sex	1
Telephone number	11

Checking data

Data is only useful as long as it is correct and up-to-date. Because of this, it is important to check data when it is entered to make sure that it is both reasonable and correct. If data is not checked before it is processed, any errors could cause the final output to be nonsense. There are two methods that can be used to check data when it is input: **verification** and **validation**.

Verification

Verification is checking to make sure data has been entered correctly. Verification is often carried out by getting two users to enter the same set of data at different computers. Once both users have entered the data, the two sets of data are compared to check that they match up. Any data that does not match up is checked. Verification can also just involve a simple visual check, where a user enters data and then compares what is on screen with what they have on paper to make sure both match up.

Validation

Validation checks are carried out by software to make sure data which has been entered is **reasonable**. Data that is not reasonable is rejected by the computer.

*In the examination you could be asked to explain what is meant by the terms **data verification** and **data validation**. Make sure that you can:*

- *explain what each of these terms means – a key point to include in your answer is that verification involves people whereas validation is carried out automatically by software;*
- *describe the different types of validation check, how they work and what type of error each can detect.*

There are many different types of validation check that software can make on data; some of these are described below.

Range check

Range checks are used to check that data is within a certain range of numbers or a specific set of values. For example if the examination marks for a group of students were being input, a range check could be used to make sure each mark was greater than or equal to zero and less than or equal to the maximum possible mark.

Figure 10.2a
A validation rule for a field in an MS Access database, to check that values input for student exam marks are between 0 and 100

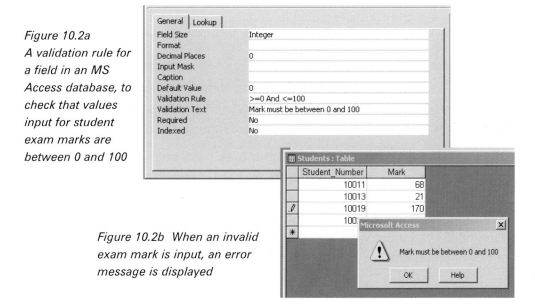

Figure 10.2b When an invalid exam mark is input, an error message is displayed

Type check

Type checks are used to check that the correct type of data has been entered in a field. For example, if numeric data is being input, a type check could be used to make sure that text data isn't entered by accident.

Figure 10.3 In this example an error message has been displayed because a user has tried to enter text data in a field where the data type is specified as integer

Parity check

Sometimes when data is being transferred electronically from one place to another it can become corrupted. A parity check is used to make sure that data has not been corrupted during transmission. Data is transmitted as a binary pattern of 0s and 1s. A parity check involves adding an extra 0 or 1, called a **parity bit**, to the binary pattern so that the total number of 1s in the pattern is either an even number, which is called **even parity**, or an odd number, which is called **odd parity**.

In even parity the parity bit is set to either 0 or 1 so that the total number of 1s adds up to an even number. In this example there are four 1s so the value 0 is needed in the parity bit to keep the number of 1s even.

In odd parity the parity bit is set to either 0 or 1 so that the total number of 1s adds up to an odd number. In this example there are two 1s so the value 1 is needed in the parity bit to make the number of 1s odd.

Figure 10.4 Parity

Hash totals

Hash totals are used to check that groups of numbers have been input correctly. A hash total is the sum of a group of numbers that are going to be input. The hash total is input along with the numbers. The computer calculates a hash total for the numbers that have been input. If the hash total calculated by the computer does not match the hash total input with the numbers then one or more of the numbers have either not been entered or have been entered incorrectly.

Another special type of hash total is called a **control total**. The difference between a hash total and a control total is that the actual value of a control total is important and means something. For example if the amounts of subscriptions paid by the members of a health club were being input, the control total would not just be a meaningless number but would represent the total amount paid by all the members.

Check digits

Check digits are used to validate long numbers that have a lot of digits in them. A check digit is an extra digit placed at the end of a long number that can be used to check if the number has been input correctly. Check digits are often used to check numbers that have been input using direct data entry devices such as barcode scanners or light pens. The value of a check digit is worked out by performing a calculation using the individual digits that make up a number. This calculation gives the value of the check digit, which is then added as an extra digit to the end of the number. Any computer can then follow the steps shown below to make sure that a number has been input correctly.

The best-known method of calculating check digits is the modulus-11 system, which traps over 99% of all errors. To calculate what a check digit should be using this system:

• each digit is assigned a weight, starting at 2 with the right-hand digit;
• each digit is multiplied by its weight;
• the results of these calculations are added together to give a total;
• the total is divided by 11;
• the remainder is subtracted from 11 to give the check digit. The two exceptions are:
  - if the remainder is 0 the result is 11 so the check digit is 0, not 11.
  - if the remainder is 1 the result is 10 so the check digit is X, not 10.

E.g., to calculate the check digit for the number 1587.

original number	1	5	8	7
weights	5	4	3	2
multiply digit by its weight	5	20	24	14
add up the results	5 + 20 + 24 + 14 = 63			
divide the total by 11	5 remainder 8			
subtract remainder from 11	11 − 8 = **3** this is the check digit			

The complete number with its check digit on the end is **15873**.

Chapter 10

Length check

Length checks are used to check that input data contains a certain number of characters. For example, if a value in a certain field had to contain five digits and only four digits were input, an error message would be given to the user.

Presence check

A presence check is used to make sure that a value has actually been entered in a field. In some database files, entering data in certain fields can be optional. Other fields, such as key fields for example, are compulsory and must have values entered in them. A presence check makes sure that data is present in a field where it is compulsory that a value be entered.

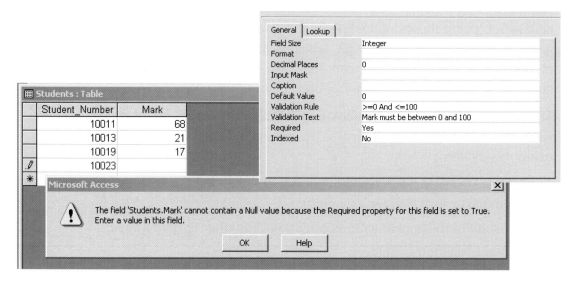

Figure 10.5 In this example an error message has been displayed because a user has not entered a value in a field where a value must be present

TIP

You could be asked to choose or suggest appropriate validation checks for some fields in a database. Make sure that you know and understand how each of the validation checks listed above works and the types of error they are used to prevent.

Coding data

When data is input using a manual input device such as a keyboard, errors often occur due to values being entered incorrectly. A common mistake is to swap two letters or digits around – this is called a **transposition error**. One method that can be used to cut down on errors like this is to use **coded values** for data. Suppose that a field could contain one of three possible values: small, medium or large. Instead of typing in the full word each time, we could instead type S, M or L.

Coding values can also lead to problems with interpretation. Suppose three colours have the codes **B**, **G**, and **P**. Do these codes stand for 'blue', 'green' and 'pink'. Or do they represent 'black', 'grey' and 'purple'? If these codes are interpreted incorrectly mistakes could be made when data is input.

You could be asked to give some advantages of coding data. Some possible answers are:

TIP

- *time is saved when entering data because there is less to type in each time;*

- *less storage space is needed because fewer characters are stored in the field;*

- *fewer key presses are needed when entering a value in the field, so there is less chance of the wrong keys being pressed;*

- *database packages allow automatic validation checks to be set up to make sure that only the permitted codes have been input to a field.*

Questions

1. A gym and health centre is about to open in early autumn. The membership secretary needs a data capture form for new members to complete. The details from the data capture form will be put into their members database.

    In the space below design **part** of the data capture form for new members. Care should be taken to include **five** suitable fields and enough space to fill in their details. (5)

    AQA 2003 Higher Tier

    Use one side of blank A4 paper for your answer to this question.

2.   (a) Fill in the gaps in the paragraph below using the words from the following list.

correct	presence	range
digit	processing	sensible
input	output	software

    Data validation is the checking of data when ...., using

    .... to make sure it is .... Two common

    methods of data validation are a .... check and a

    .... check.

    (5)

    (b) Why is the use of data validation so important? (2)

    AQA (NEAB) 2000 Paper 1 Tier H

3.   (a) Give **two** advantages of *coding* data. (2)

    (b) Explain why coding data can sometimes lead to problems. (2)

4. Explain how each of the methods listed below can be used for data validation.

    (a) Parity check (3)

    (b) Type check (2)

    (c) Hash total (2)

    (d) Range check (2)

Web tasks

1. Visit the Free On-Line Dictionary of Computing (FOLDOC) at:
    http://wombat.doc.ic.ac.uk/foldoc/

    (a) Look up definitions of the keywords highlighted in this chapter.

    (b) Prepare a summary list of keywords and definitions to use for revision.

2. Visit **http://support.microsoft.com/?kbid=311167**

    Use the **Microsoft Knowledge Base** articles to prepare a summary of the facilities, including data validation, offered by MS Access that can be used to help keep information accurate.

    Note: If you use a different database package at school, carry out your own research and write about this.

The **Police National Computer**, or **PNC** for short, is a mainframe computer used by every police force in the UK. The PNC was set up over thirty years ago and initially contained just one database of information about stolen vehicles. Today the PNC is connected to 10,000 terminals across the country and holds multiple databases on criminals, vehicles and property.

Vehicle Online Descriptive Search

Police officers investigating crimes often have descriptions of vehicles from witnesses, which they can use to identify potential suspects. The **Vehicle Online Descriptive Search (VODS)** allows operators to enter a partial description of a vehicle and search a database of over 50 million records for matches. Descriptions can include any combination of the make, model, colour, year of registration, or engine capacity of a vehicle. Before VODS was introduced, this type of search could take hours or even days.

Figure CS2.1 VODS allows the operator to enter a partial description of a vehicle and search a database of over 50 million records for matches

Drivers

The PNC holds databases that provide police officers with information at the roadside on drivers, motor insurance and vehicle MOTs. When officers stop a vehicle they radio a local police control room to request a check on both the driver and vehicle. This is to make sure the driver is not disqualified from driving or wanted in connection with another crime, and to check the vehicle they are driving is properly insured and legal to drive. Previously when drivers were stopped by the police they would be given seven days to produce their driving licence, insurance documents and MOT certificate in person at a police station. This system was very time-consuming for police officers and inconvenient for drivers.

Figure CS2.2 (a) When police officers stop a vehicle they radio the local control room to carry out a roadside check on the driver

Figure CS2.2 (b) Police officers at the local control room check the information given by the driver against records held in PNC databases

Automatic Number Plate Recognition

Automatic Number Plate Recognition (ANPR) cameras scan and store thousands of vehicle registration numbers every hour. The recognition time of ANPR systems is typically less than one second and is 99.9% accurate. Numbers collected by police ANPR systems are checked against PNC and local databases to identify vehicles of interest to officers. If a registration number is matched against a database record, the system alerts the ANPR operator, who can call for officers to intercept the vehicle and question the driver.

Automatic Number Plate Recognition is used in London to combat crime and terrorism. The number plates of vehicles going in and out of the City's square mile are automatically scanned and checked against PNC databases. When a match is found, police officers are sent to intercept the suspect vehicle and question the occupants. Crime in the City of London has dropped considerably since the introduction of this system.

Figure CS2.3 Automatic Number Plate Recognition Software

In this example, APNR software and CCTV cameras are being used to identify cars entering a car park. The software 'reads' the licence plate, signals to the parking gate, and keeps a record of the entry and exit times for automatic payment calculations

National Automated Fingerprint Identification System

Fingerprints are permanent, unique and identify us as individuals. The use of fingerprints to identify criminals was introduced in 1889. The traditional method of identification using fingerprints is very slow and time-consuming. It involves using a magnifying glass to look for similarities between a set of suspect fingerprints and those held in paper-based records.

The **National Automated Fingerprint Identification System (NAFIS)** allows scanned images of fingerprints taken from suspects and crime scenes to be compared against a national database of over five million sets of fingerprints held on the PNC. Possible matches are returned within seconds. Before NAFIS was introduced, all fingerprint searches were carried out at New Scotland Yard and often took weeks or even months to complete.

Fingerprints can now be captured by direct electronic scanning. Twenty-seven UK police forces are currently using this technology. This method of taking fingerprints allows them to be transmitted directly to NAFIS as digital images, and makes the almost instant identification of suspects possible. Many countries, including the UK and the USA, are planning to introduce this type of system at airports to identify travellers and help combat terrorism.

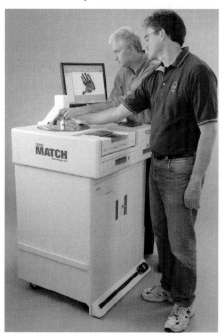

Figure CS2.4 The electronic scanning of fingerprints
This system can directly scan finger and palm prints – smaller versions of this type of device
are being introduced by police forces across the UK

Home Office Large Major Enquiry System

The **Home Office Large Major Enquiry System** (or **HOLMES** for short) is used by the police to help with long and complicated investigations like murder enquiries. Before HOLMES, forces had to manage huge amounts of information by hand. The HOLMES system reduces paperwork and releases officers to spend more time actually working on solving crimes. When a serious crime or incident takes place the HOLMES system:

- collates and analyses information fed into the incident room;
- identifies and plots new lines of enquiry for detectives to follow up;
- keeps track of evidence as it is collected and stored.

Sometimes it is necessary for more than one incident room to be set up in different parts of the country. HOLMES is also very useful in situations like this because it allows different police forces to work together by entering information into one central HOLMES database.

HOLMES is also used to help co-ordinate the aftermath of major incidents such as terrorist attacks, natural disasters or accidents. When a serious incident takes place, the police receive thousands of telephone calls from anxious relatives about missing family members. The HOLMES system is used to match information given by these callers to casualty details. Once matches are confirmed, relatives are contacted straight away. HOLMES was used in this way after the September 11th terrorist attacks in the United States. The system helped government agencies to identify British victims by matching UK missing person reports with US casualty lists.

DNA profiling

DNA profiling, (or **genetic fingerprinting**), is becoming an increasingly important crime-detection tool for the police. The cells in our bodies contain a unique genetic material called DNA, which can be used to identify individuals with much more certainty than fingerprints. Scientists have estimated that there is a fifty million to one chance of any two people having the same DNA profile. The **Forensic Science Service (FSS)** maintains a database of DNA samples taken from known criminals, suspects and crime scenes. Identifications are made by taking a sample of a suspect's DNA and searching the FSS database for a matching record.

Questions

1. Describe **two** ways ICT systems are used by the police to help reduce paperwork. (4)

2.   (a) What do the letters **NAFIS** stand for? (1)

       (b) Explain how the police use NAFIS help them to solve crimes. (2)

       (c) Describe one other possible use of this type of system. (2)

3. The **Home Office Large Major Enquiry System** (or **HOLMES** for short) is used by the police to help with long and complicated investigations like murder enquiries.

       (a) Give **three** functions carried out by the HOLMES system. (3)

       (b) Describe **one** other way HOLMES is used by the police. (2)

4. Explain briefly how DNA profiling can help with serious crime investigations. (3)

Web tasks

1. The London congestion charge is another example of how ANPR technology is being used. Visit the Transport for London website at:

   www.tfl.gov.uk/tfl/cclondon/cc_fact_sheet.shtml

   Use the information you find to prepare a short presentation describing the role of ANPR in the London congestion charging scheme. You should make sure your presentation also describes **at least one** other application of ANPR .

2. Electronic fingerprint scanning is just one of the **biometric identification methods** being introduced by governments to help combat crime and terrorism. Visit the Forensic-Evidence.com site at:

   www.forensic-evidence.com/site/ID/ID_Biometric_jarvis.html

   Use the information and links on this site to prepare a presentation about the different **biometric identification methods** available and how they are being used. Your presentation should end by outlining some of the new techniques currently under development.

Spreadsheets

A **spreadsheet package** is a general purpose computer package that is designed to perform **calculations**. A spreadsheet is a table which is divided into **rows** and **columns**. Columns have a letter at the top and rows have a number at the side. Lines divide the rows and columns up into boxes called **cells**. A cell can contain **text**, a **number** or a **formula**. An individual cell is identified by its **cell reference number**, which normally contains a column letter and a row number.

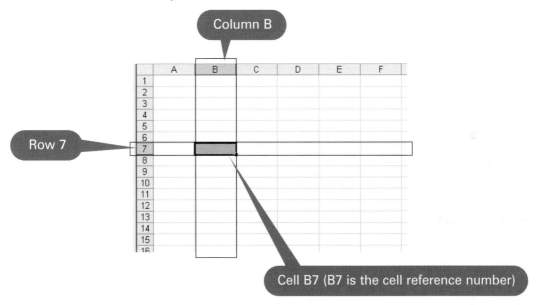

Figure 11.1 The parts of a spreadsheet

Formulae

A **formula** is used on a spreadsheet to perform a calculation using the numbers in other cells. The result of the calculation is displayed in the cell where the formula has been entered.

A simple formula can be used to add, subtract, multiply or divide numbers. To carry out these sorts of calculation, the symbols below are used:

+   to **add**

-      to **subtract**

*   to **multiply**

/   to **divide**

Suppose, for example, that you wanted to add two numbers on a spreadsheet together. If the numbers were in cells **A1** and **A2** then the formula that you would need to enter would be something like this:

$$= A1+A2$$

You would need to enter this formula in the cell where you wanted the answer to appear. The "=" sign at the beginning of the formula is there to tell the spreadsheet package that what's been entered is a formula. Some spreadsheet packages use a different symbol to do this.

When a new spreadsheet is being set up, very similar formulae are often needed in adjacent cells. If this is the case, a single formula can be copied or replicated into adjacent cells. The spreadsheet software will automatically update the cell references in the original formula so that the new formulae refer to the correct cells.

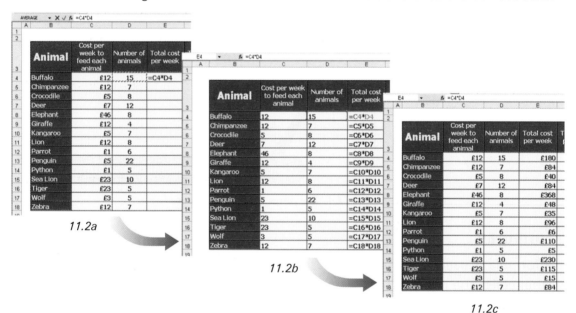

11.2a

11.2b

11.2c

Figure 11.2 Replicating a formula
is a quick way to set up a spreadsheet

Sometimes when a formula is replicated the cell references in some parts of the formula do not need to be changed – instead they need to refer to the same cells in each of the new formulae. In situations like this an **absolute cell reference** must be used. Absolute cell references in a formula 'lock' individual cell references so that they remain the same whenever the formula is replicated. To set up an absolute cell reference, $ signs are normally placed to the left of the numbers and letters in the cell reference.

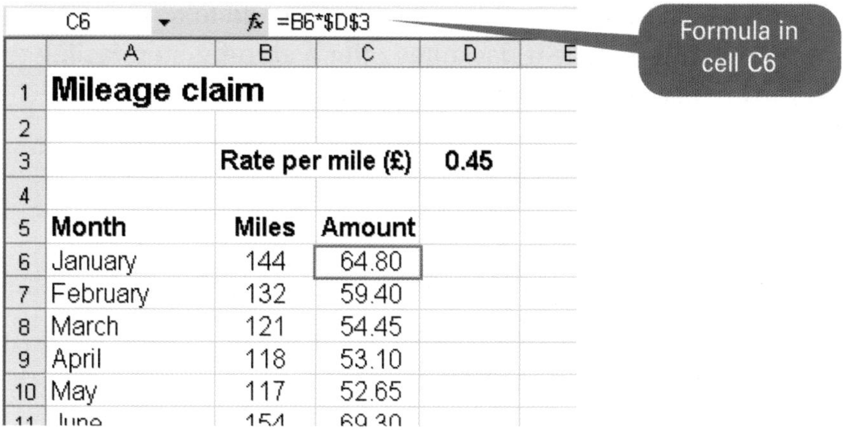

	A	B	C	D	E
1	**Mileage claim**				
2					
3		**Rate per mile (£)**		**0.45**	
4					
5	**Month**	**Miles**	**Amount**		
6	January	144	64.80		
7	February	132	59.40		
8	March	121	54.45		
9	April	118	53.10		
10	May	117	52.65		

Figure 11.3 Absolute cell references are normally specified using $ signs

Functions

To make it easier to enter a longer, more complicated formula, spreadsheet packages also have special **mathematical functions** built in. Two of the most commonly used functions are the **SUM** or **AVERAGE** of a range of cells. Suppose, for example, that you had a formula like this:

=A1+A2+A3+A4+A5+A6+A7+A8+A9+A10

This formula would add up all the numbers in cells A1 to A10. Instead of typing in such a long formula, the **SUM** function could be used. On most spreadsheets the formula would be something like this:

= **SUM (A1: A10)**

If a number of cells need the same formula it can be copied and pasted in the same way as text.

Similarly, to work out the average of the numbers in cells A1 to A10, the **AVERAGE** function could be used. On most spreadsheets the formula would be something like this:

= **AVERAGE (A1: A10)**

Exactly what you need to type in will depend upon the spreadsheet package that you are using.

Some built-in spreadsheet functions can be quite complicated and difficult to use. Most good spreadsheet packages offer a step-by-step facility to help users build formulae that include functions.

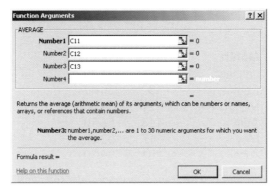

Figure 11.4 The Insert Function facility in MS Excel helps users to enter
formulae containing functions

Cell formatting

Spreadsheet packages, like word processing packages, have built-in formatting options – called **cell formats** – which allow you to change the way a spreadsheet looks by changing the appearance of cells or their contents. Some of the cell formats that a good spreadsheet package should offer are described below.

Changing font size and style

The style of text in a cell can be changed. Different styles of text are called **fonts** (there's more about this in the next chapter). The size of text in individual cells or groups of cells can be changed. In most spreadsheet packages **bold**, *italic*, underlined and different-coloured text can also be used.

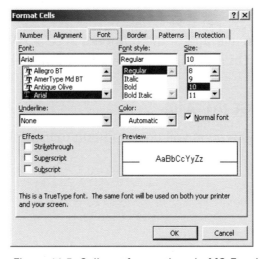

Figure 11.5 Cell text font options in MS Excel

Changing text alignment

The position of text in a cell can be changed using **text alignment** formats. Text can be aligned **vertically** or **horizontally**. The contents of a cell can be horizontally aligned **left**, **right**, or in the **centre**.

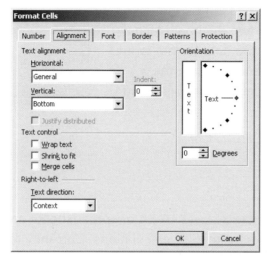

Figure 11.6 Cell text alignment options in MS Excel

Borders and lines

Individual cells or groups of cells can have borders drawn around them. In most spreadsheet packages both the style, thickness and colour of the line can be changed.

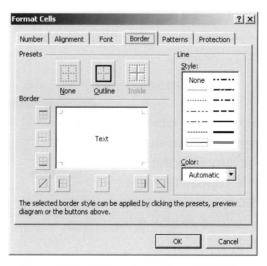

Figure 11.7 Cell border options in MS Excel

Decimal

Decimal data format is used when a number needs a decimal point in it. When using decimal format, the required number of decimal places must be chosen by the user. For example, to display two decimal places after the decimal point, the data format would be '**0.00**' or '**#.##**' depending upon the particular spreadsheet package that is being used.

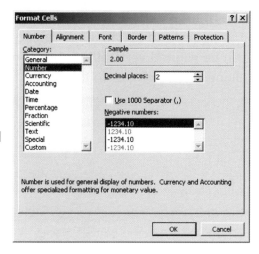

Figure 11.8 Specifying decimal data format

Currency

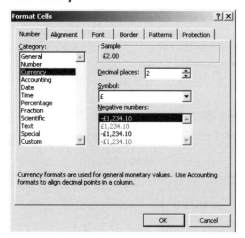

A lot of spreadsheets are used for financial calculations. Currency format is used to display a **£**, **€** or **$** symbol in front of a number. The required number of decimal places (normally 2 or 0) can be specified in the currency format.

Figure 11.9 Specifying currency data format

Date

Date format is used in cells where dates have been entered, to specify the way that the date should be displayed; for example, a date format of **dd-mm-yy** would display the date **12th June 2004** as **12-06-04**, whereas a date format of **dd-mmm-yyyy**, would display the same date as **12-Jun-2004**.

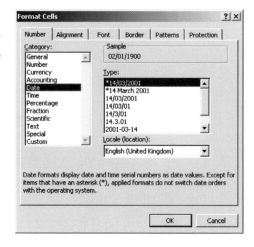

Figure 11.10 Specifying date format

Inserting extra rows and columns

Sometimes, when working on a spreadsheet, it becomes necessary to insert an extra row or an extra column. Most spreadsheets allow you to do this quite easily. When an extra row or column is inserted, the spreadsheet automatically updates the cell references in any formulae that are affected by the change.

Changing column width and row height

The size of a cell depends upon the width of the column that it is in and the height of the row that it is in. When any spreadsheet is being set up for the first time, all the columns and rows have the same width and height, which means that all the cells are the same size. At this stage, the size of the cells is said to be set to the **default value**. When data is entered into a cell it might not fit into the size allowed by the default value. If this is the case, the column width can be adjusted by the user until the data fits in the cell. Similarly, if a row is too narrow (or too high), its height can be altered by the user. Some spreadsheets can be set up to automatically adjust the column width when data is entered. Such an option is normally called **best-fit** or **auto-size**.

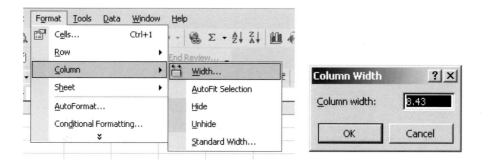

Figure 11.11 Setting column width in MS Excel

Sorting data

One very useful feature of a spreadsheet package is the **sort** facility. This allows the columns or rows of a spreadsheet to be sorted into **alphabetical** or **numerical** order of the values in a particular row or column.

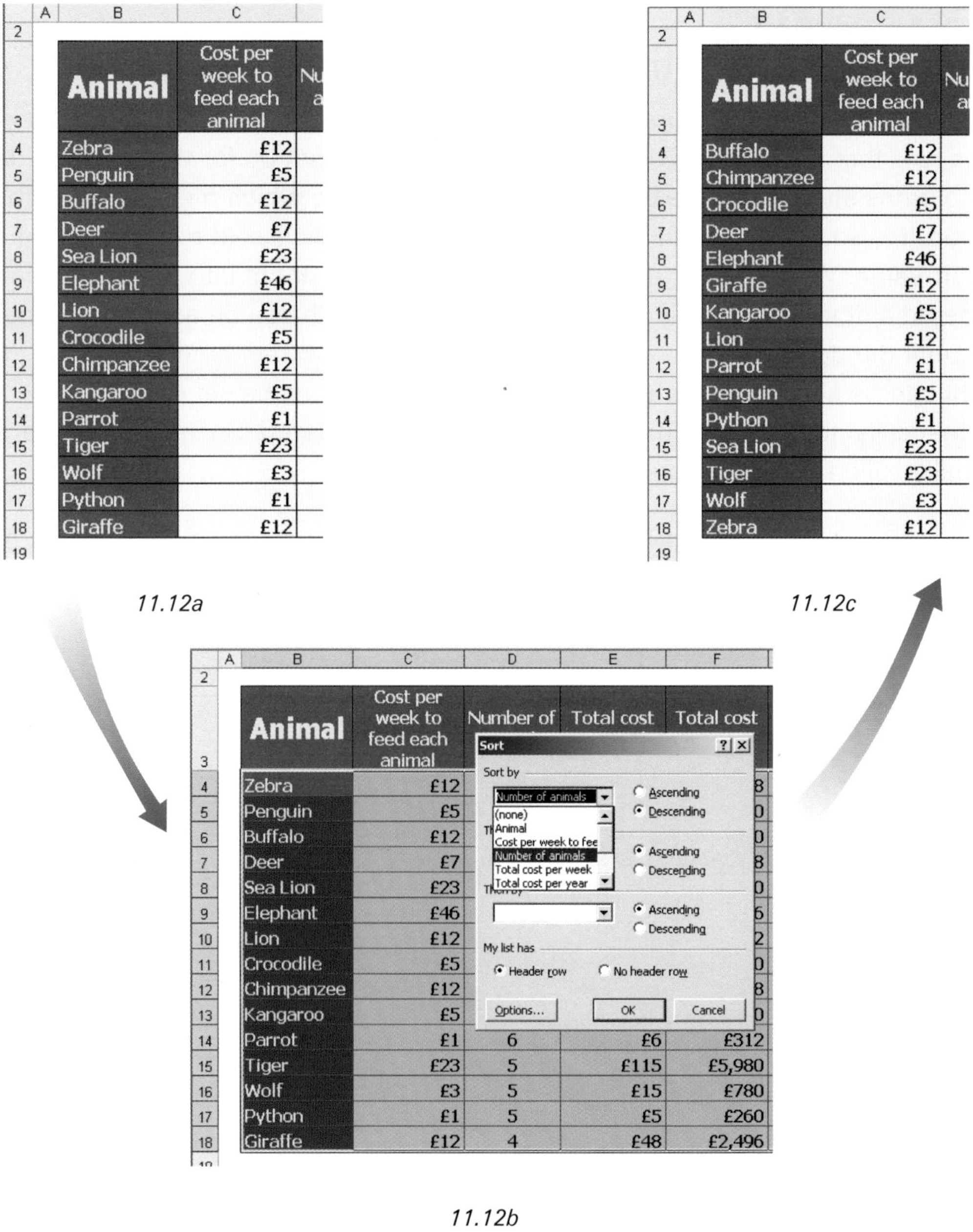

11.12a

11.12c

11.12b

Figure 11.12 Sorting data in MS Excel

Graphs and charts

Most spreadsheet packages include facilities for representing information in the form of a graph or chart. The most common types are bar charts, pie charts and line graphs. A chart wizard gives step-by-step help when drawing a graph or chart.

The first step in creating a graph or chart is to set up the spreadsheet and highlight the data that needs to be represented in the graph or chart.

	A	B	C	D	E	F
1	Title: Visits to the UK by overseas residents,1978 to 1999					
2						
3	Year	Business visits	Holiday visits	Miscellaneous	Visiting friends or relatives	Total visits
4	1978	2295	5876	2283	2193	12647
5	1979	2395	5529	2308	2254	12486
6	1980	2565	5478	2058	2319	12420
7	1981	2453	5037	1675	2287	11452
8	1982	2393	5265	1568	2410	11636
9	1983	2556	5818	1530	2560	12464
10	1984	2863	6385	1770	2626	13644
11	1985	3014	6666	1890	2880	14450
12	1986	3286	5919	1746	2946	13897
13	1987	3564	6828	1996	3179	15567
14	1988	4096	6655	1870	3178	15799
15	1989	4363	7286	2193	3497	17339
16	1990	4461	7725	2216	3611	18013
17	1991	4219	7169	2147	3591	17126
18	1992	3855	7949	2847	3884	18535
19	1993	4706	8729	2319	4109	19863
20	1994	4986	9048	2482	4278	20794
21	1995	5763	10323	2849	4602	23537
22	1996	6095	10987	3182	4898	25162
23	1997	6347	10803	3209	5155	25514
24	1998	6882	10475	2988	5400	25745
25	1999	7044	9826	2884	5640	25394
26	Total	90201	165776	50010	77497	383484

11.13a

The next step is to choose the type of graph or chart.

11.13b

The graph or chart is automatically drawn by the spreadsheet software. It can then be copied and pasted into other applications if required.

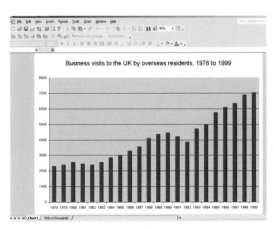

11.13c

Figure 11.13 Using the chart wizard in MS Excel

Questions

1. Mr Osman uses a spreadsheet to plan his monthly spending. The spreadsheet is shown below

	A	B	C
1	**Monthly expenses**		
2			
3	**Total income for the month**	£1250	
4			
5	**Item**	**Amount**	
6	Food	240.00	
7	Gas	15.00	
8	Electricity	20.00	
9	Water	7.00	
10	Council tax	78.00	
11	Travel to work	100.00	
12	Entertainment	280.00	
13	**Total outgoing**	£740.00	
14			
15	**Savings**	£510.00	

(a) (i) Give the **address** of the **cell** whose contents would have to be changed if the monthly cost of electricity increased. (1)

    (ii) Give the **addresses** of **two cells** whose contents would change automatically as a result. (2)

(b) State the **formulas** contained in the following cells.

    (i) **B13**

    (ii) **B15** (2)

(c) Give **four cell formats** that have been used in this spreadsheet (4)

2. You have been asked to plan a friend's birthday party. To help investigate the cost of the party you have set up the spreadsheet shown below.

	A	B	C
1	**Number of guests**	60	
2			
3	**Item**		Cost
4	Room hire		£100
5	Buffet (per person)	£3.25	£195
6	Disco		£150
7		**Total cost**	**£445**

(a) Write down the **address** of the **cell** that contains the cost of room hire. (1)

(b) Write down the **formula** that would be entered in cell **C5**. (1)

(c) Write down the **formula** that would be entered in cell **C7**. (1)

(d) You have decided to investigate the effects of changing the number of guests. Write down the **address** of the **cell** whose contents will need to be changed. (1)

(e) Changing the number in this cell would also cause the numbers in **two** other cells to change. Write down the **addresses** of these **cells**. (1)

(f) What **data format** has been used for the **Cost** column? (1)

(g) What **data format** has been used in cell **B5**? (1)

3. (a) Describe the **cell** and **data formatting** features that have been used in the spreadsheet shown below. (10)

	A	B	C	D	E	F	G
1	Supermarket Price Comparison						
2							
3		BACON	BREAD	CHEESE	EGGS	MILK	
4	Product Size	425g	Medium Loaf	425g	Dozen	1 Pint	
5							Total Cost
6	Bettabuys	1.98	0.65	2.25	1.09	0.35	£6.32
7	Cheapco	2.27	0.62	2.62	1.21	0.32	£7.04
8	SuperSaver	2.09	0.61	2.18	1.05	0.34	£6.27
9							
10	Average Cost	£2.11	£0.63	£2.35	£1.12	£0.34	£6.54
11							

(b) Write down the **formula** that has been used to calculate the value shown in cell **B10**. (2)

(c) Write down the **formula** that has been used to calculate the value shown in cell **G6**. (2)

4. A school has decided to extend its computer network. The headteacher uses software to help him work out the cost. His first attempt is given below.

	A	B	C	D	E	F
1	Item to be bought	Unit cost	No. to	Total cost	Discount	Total cost
2			buy	before discount		after discount
3						
4	Computer	£399.00	40	£15 960.00	10%	£14 364.00
5	15" monitor	£90.00	40	£3 600.00	10%	£3 240.00
6	Laser printer	£450.00	2	£900.00	0%	£900.00
7	Colour printer	£250.00	1	£250.00	0%	£250.00
8	Electronic whiteboard	£4 000.00	2	£8 000.00	5%	£7 600.00
9	Network points	£50.00	40	£2 000.00	15%	£1 700.00
10	Software licences	£170.00	40	£6 800.00	20%	£5 440.00
11						
12					Total	£33 494.00

(a) Tick **one** box to show which type of software package has been used.

	Tick **one** box
Spreadsheet	
Desk Top Publishing	
Communications	
CAD	

(1)

(b) State the formulas which would be contained in the following cells.

   (i) **D4**

   (ii) **F4**

   (iii) **F12**

(3)

(c) Tick **one** box to show which word describes the data in the highlighted cell **C5**.

	Tick **one** box
Text	
Numeric	
Formula	
Date	

(1)

(d) The headteacher has only £30 000 to spend. He can reduce the cost to less than £30 000 by reducing the number of software licences he buys. Why would this not be a sensible thing for him to do? (1)

(e) Tick **three** boxes to show the advantages to the headteacher of using this software package to help him work out the cost, rather than using a calculator and paper.

	Tick **3** boxes only
Easier to edit	
The computers will arrive faster	
He will get a bigger discount	
Changes are automatically re-calculated in the totals	
Time can be saved by replication of cells	
He does not need to do any work	

(3)

(f) Describe **two** possible disadvantages to the headteacher of using this software package to help him work out the cost rather than using a calculator and paper. (2)

AQA (NEAB) Paper 1 2001 Tier H

5. Mrs Brown uses a spreadsheet to help her calculate the cost of decorating and buying some new furniture for her son's bedroom. Her first attempt is shown below.

	A	B	C	D	E	F	G
1	Item to be purchased	Unit cost	Number needed	Total cost per item			
2							
3	Wallpaper (per roll)	£6.95	6	£41.70			
4	Wallpaper paste (per packet)	£2.99	2	£5.98			
5	Paint (per tin) - red	£4.49	2	£8.98			
6	Paint (per tin) - white	£3.99	3	£11.97			
7	Paintbrush	£1.49	3	£4.47			
8	Carpet (per sq metre)	£12.99	9	£116.91			
9	Lampshade	£8.50	2	£17.00			
10	Quilt	£22.99	2	£45.98			
11	Quilt cover	£17.25	3	£51.75			
12	Curtains (pair)	£34.45	2	£68.90			
13	Wardrobe	£99.99	2	£199.98			
14	Bed	£199.99	1	£199.99			
15	Computer desk	£199.00	1	£199.00			
16	Chest of drawers	£33.75	3	£101.25			
17							
18	Total cost for the bedroom			£1,073.86			

(a) Which cell contains the unit cost of a paintbrush?

	Tick **one** box only
A6	
B6	
A7	
B7	

(1)

(b) All the cells in this spreadsheet contain either text, number or formulae.

State which **one** of these is contained in the following cells:

(i) B14

(ii) A14

(2)

(c) State the formula which would be contained in each of the following cells:

(i) D3

(ii) D18 (2)

(d) Mrs Brown has only £550 to spend on the bedroom. Explain clearly how she could use the spreadsheet to investigate "what if" situations to help her keep within her budget. (2)

AQA 2003 (Short Course) Higher Tier

Web tasks

1. Visit the Free On-Line Dictionary of Computing (FOLDOC) at:
    http://wombat.doc.ic.ac.uk/foldoc/

    (a) Look up definitions of the keywords highlighted in this chapter.

    (b) Prepare a summary list of keywords and definitions to use for revision.

2. If you use MS Excel at school or home visit the **PCWorld.com** website at:
    www.pcworld.com/howto/article/0,aid,105312,00.asp

    Check out the top ten Excel tips and try any that you don't already know about.

3. Visit the **About.com** website at:

    http://spreadsheets.about.com/library/weekly/blexformquiz.htm

    Take the quiz there to test your spreadsheet design and formatting knowledge.

4. Find out more about MS Excel functions at:

    www.meadinkent.co.uk/excel.htm

A word processor is used to **write**, **edit**, **format** and **print** text. Before word processors, printed documents were typed directly onto paper using manual typewriters.

Figure 12.1 A manual typewriter

The main problem with using manual typewriters was that when mistakes were made they could not be corrected without leaving any trace. Often, if a typist made a mistake, the entire document would have to be typed out again. This made the process of producing printed documents very time-consuming. Word processing software was developed to overcome this problem. This chapter describes the typical features offered by good word processing application packages that can be used to improve the appearance of printed documents.

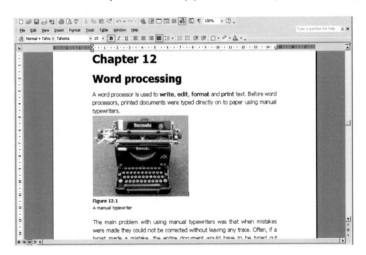

Figure 12.2 MS Word: a popular word processing application package

Font style and size

The size of text is changed by adjusting the **point size**. The larger the point size, the bigger the text will be.

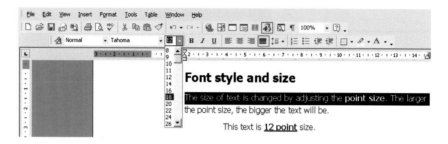

Figure 12.3 *Changing the point size of text in MS Word*

The appearance of text is changed by choosing a different **font style**. Word processing packages offer many fonts each with their own name – some examples of this are shown below.

This font is called Comic Sans

This font is called Tahoma

This font is called Papyrus

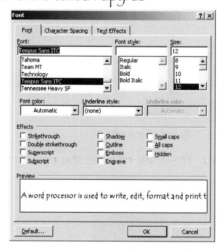

Figure 12.4 *Changing font style in MS Word*

Other effects that can be used to change the appearance of text are options to make it **bold**, *italic* or <u>underlined</u>. Word processing packages often collect similar functions like these together on a **toolbar** to make them easier to use.

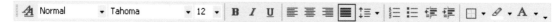

Figure 12.5 *The Formatting toolbar of MS Word*

Cutting and pasting

The **cut** facility of a word processor allows users to choose part of the text and 'cut it out'. 'Cut' text can either be thrown away or **pasted** somewhere else in the same – or another – document.

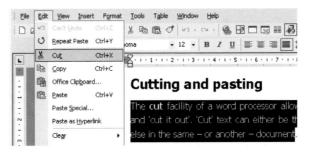

Figure 12.6 Cutting text in MS Word

The **copy** facility allows you to choose part of your text and then paste a copy of it elsewhere in your document. The cut, copy and paste facilities of a word processor also work with graphics.

Figure 12.7 Copying text in MS Word

Tabulation

Tabulation allows the **tab key** to be set to jump forward a pre-set distance across a page each time it is pressed. The user can set the distance that the tab key will jump to any value they want.

Figure 12.8 Setting the tab key stop position in MS Word

Tabulation is used to align or indent text on a page.

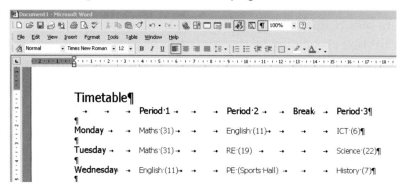

Figure 12.9 The text in this example has been arranged in columns using tabs. All the text in each column is lined up with a tab stop along the ruler line. The tab stops are shown by the small arrows – these are not usually visible in a document

Word-wrap

Word-wrap means that when you are typing you do not have to press the enter key at the end of a line; the word processor will begin a new line whenever one is needed. The Enter key is pressed only to start a new paragraph or to leave a deliberate gap of one or more lines between blocks of text.

Search and replace

Search and replace allows you to tell the word processor to look for one word and replace it with another. This can be done **selectively** for just part of a document or **globally**. Selective search and replace will check each time it finds the search word whether or not you want to replace it. Global search and replace finds every occurrence of the search word and replaces it without asking first.

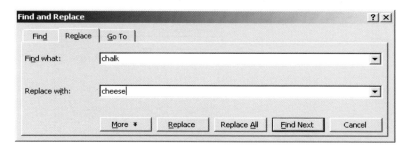

Figure 12.10 Using search and replace in MS Word. In this example the user wants the word 'chalk' replaced by the word 'cheese'

Line spacing

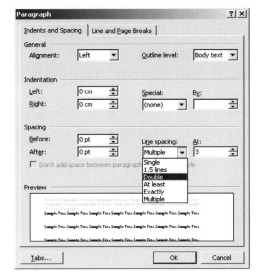

Line spacing is used to change the amount of space between lines of text. Normal text is single spaced. Common line spacing options include 'single', '1.5 times', and 'double'.

Figure 12.11 Some of the line spacing options available in MS Word

You can also change the space between lines by adjusting the '**leading**'. This term originates from the days when typesetters placed strips of lead (metal) between lines of text created from individual metal letters. The finished plate was then inked and used to print books and newspapers. The lines in this block of text are **double spaced**.

Margins

The **margin** settings for a document determine how much blank space must be left between the text and the page edges. Changing the margin settings is one method that can be used to fit more text on each page of a document.

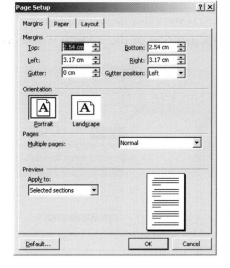

Figure 12.12 Changing page margin settings in MS Word

Spelling and grammar checkers

A **spell checker** uses a built-in dictionary to check the spellings in your text. When a spell checker finds words that are unknown, it will offer possible alternatives from its dictionary and ask if you want to choose a replacement, delete the unknown word completely, keep the word as it is, or enter your own alternative word. Spell checkers are not foolproof, however, and you do need to have a reasonable knowledge of correct spellings; otherwise you might end up choosing incorrect alternative words as corrections, making your finished text read very strangely indeed.

A **grammar checker** uses a built-in set of 'rules' about the grammar of the language that you are using. Grammar checkers **do not** check spellings; they just check that what you have written follows the rules of a language correctly.

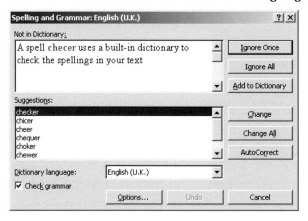

Figure 12.13 Using the combined spelling and grammar checker in MS Word

In this example the dialogue box shows an incorrect spelling and possible words to use as corrections

Thesaurus

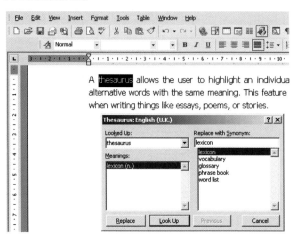

A thesaurus allows the user to highlight an individual word and see a list of alternative words with the same meaning. This feature can be particularly useful when writing things like essays, poems, or stories.

Figure 12.14 Using the thesaurus in MS Word. The thesaurus is used by highlighting a word then pressing the Shift and F7 keys together

Import and export

One of the major advantages that modern word processors have over typewriters is that they allow you to **import** graphics and combine graphics with text. What this means is that diagrams and pictures produced using other software packages can be included on the page along with your text.

Figure 12.15 Using the import facility in MS Word

The **export** facility is simply the opposite of import. Export allows you to transfer work produced using the word processor into other software packages.

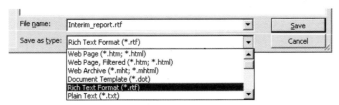

Figure 12.16 Using the export facility in MS Word

Alignment

Alignment is a feature which adds extra spaces to a block of text to line it up in a particular way. Text can be **left aligned**, **right aligned**, **centred** or **justified**.

Figure 12.17 The text alignment buttons on the formatting toolbar in MS Word

The examples below show you what the different sorts of alignment look like.

The text below is **left aligned**. This means that each line of text is lined up on the left hand side only.

"It was the best of times, it was the worst of times, it was the age of wisdom, it was the age of foolishness, it was the epoch of belief, it was the epoch of incredulity, it was the season of Light."

The text below **justified**. This means that each line of text is lined up on both the left and right hand sides.

It was the season before of Darkness, it was the spring of hope, it was the winter of despair, we had everything before us, we had nothing before us, we were all going direct to heaven, we were all going direct the other way.

The text below is **centred**. This means that each line of text is lined up in the centre of the page.

– in short, the period was so far like the present period, that some of its noisiest authorities insisted on its being received, for good or for evil, in the superlative degree of comparison only."

The text below is **right aligned**. This means that each line of text is lined up on the right hand side only.

A Tale of Two Cities
By Charles Dickens

Mail merging

Mail merging is a special feature that is included in most modern word processing packages. It allows the user to create a **standard letter** and then merge it with data from a spreadsheet, database or other text file, called the **source data file**. During the merging process, data from fields in individual records in the source data file is inserted into spaces that have been specially marked in the standard letter so a 'personalised' letter is produced for each record in the source data file. Mail merging is a very quick method of producing letters which each contain virtually the same information except for the names and addresses. Only one standard letter has to be written in order to produce many mail-merged copies. This is how many businesses send out 'direct mail' or ('junk mail') to people.

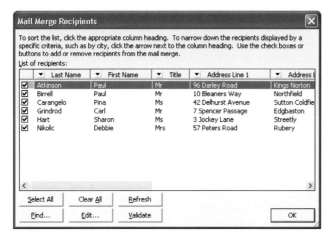

Figure 12.18a The process of mail merging in MS Word

A source data file is either prepared or imported from an existing file.

A standard letter is written and 'markers' are placed in it to indicate where data from the source file is to be inserted into each individual letter.

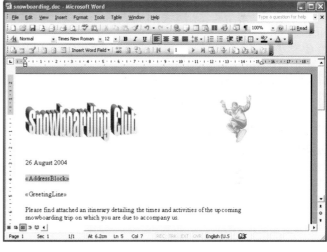

Figure 12.18b

The standard letter is merged with data from the source data file to produce individual letters.

Figure 12.18c

Using a word processor to produce printed text has many advantages when compared with older manual methods such as using a typewriter. You could be asked to give some of these advantages in the examination. Some possible answers are:

- *mistakes can be corrected easily without leaving any trace;*

- *much better presentation of text is possible with formatting features such as different font styles and sizes, coloured text and justification;*

- *text can be easily inserted, deleted or rearranged without having to start again;*

- *documents can be saved on disk and used again whenever necessary;*

- *pictures, graphs, tables and charts can be easily included alongside text;*

- *multiple copies of the same document can be easily produced;*

- *standard letters can be mass-produced very quickly using mail merge;*

- *documents can be transferred instantly anywhere in the world using electronic communications such as e-mail;*

- *spelling and grammar can be checked automatically.*

Questions

1. Mail merge is a feature that is included with most word processing packages.

    (a) Describe the steps involved in carrying out a **mail merge**. (3)

    (b) Describe **one** possible way that a business could use a mail merge facility. (1)

    (c) Give **two** advantages of using a mail merge facility. (2)

2. The school secretary used a word processing package to produce tickets for the end of term disco. Her first version of the ticket is given below.

    > **End of term Dsco**
    > Starts — 7pm Ends — 10pm
    > Cost £2
    > Venue — Sports Hall

    (a) The ticket contains the word Dsco rather than the word Disco. Which feature of the word processing package would identify this error? (1)

    (b) What other very important piece of information has been missed off the ticket? (1)

    (c) Give **five** features of the word processing package that could be used to improve the presentation of the ticket. (5)

    (d) Chose **one** of the features **given in (c) above** and give a reason why it would improve the presentation of the ticket. (1)

    (e) The Headteacher wants the secretary to use the word processing package to put each pupil's name on the ticket. Which feature of the package would she use to do this? (1)

    AQA (NEAB) 2002 Paper 1 Tier H

3. A GCSE Examination Board has started to redesign its Coursework Cover Sheet for candidates. The first attempt at the form is shown below.

Coursework Cover Sheet (GCSE)

Syllabus   ....

Subject   ....

Name of Centre   ....

Candidate's surname   ....

Other names   ....

TITLE OR DESCRIPTION OF COURSEWORK

....

....

....

SOURCES OF ADVICE AND INFORMATION

....

....

....

(a) Tick **three** boxes to show which of the following features of a word processing package could be used to improve the **layout** of the form.

	Tick **three** boxes only
Line Spacing	
Alteration of margins	
Mail-merging	
Spell checking	
Change text size	
Saving	

(3)

(b) Describe **three** other features of a word processing package which could be used to further improve the **presentation** of the form. Give an example of how each feature might be used. (6)

(c) The examination board is not happy with the order of the lines given below.

TITLE OR DESCRIPTION OF COURSEWORK

....

....

....

SOURCES OF ADVICE AND INFORMATION

....

....

....

It wants to change the layout of these lines to:

SOURCES OF ADVICE AND INFORMATION

....

....

....

TITLE OR DESCRIPTION OF COURSEWORK

....

....

....

Describe a **good** way for them to do this using the word processing package. (3)

AQA (Short Course) 2001 Tier H

4. A school secretary has prepared the letter shown below using a word processing package on one of the computers in the office.

   (a) Describe **three** improvements that could be made to the letter and the features of the word processing package that should be used to make them. (6)

   (b) Give **three** advantages of producing the letter using a word processing package rather than a manual typewriter. (3)

The Dene School
Woodlands Road
Great Grampton
GG1 2WT

Tel: (01725) 263547

Dear Parents,
As we look forward to Christmad and the end of the autumn term, I am pleased to announce that our annual Chritmas Concert will be taking place on Thursday 12th December. Tickets for this event are free but nubers are strictly limited. If you would like to come to the concert tickets can be picked up from the school office. I look forward to seeing you at the concert.

Yourd sincerely,
Mrs E. Hicks
Head Teachr

Web tasks

1. Visit the Free On-Line Dictionary of Computing (FOLDOC) at:
   http://wombat.doc.ic.ac.uk/foldoc/

   (a) Look up definitions of the keywords highlighted in this chapter.

   (b) Prepare a summary list of keywords and definitions to use for revision.

2. If you use MS Word at school or home visit the **PCWorld.com** website at:

   http://www.pcworld.com/howto/article/0,aid,88664,00.asp

   Check out the top ten Word tips and try any that you don't already know.

3. Visit the **About.com** website at:

   http://wordprocessing.about.com/library/WordTutorials/blMailmergeintro.htm

   • Read through the guide to using the MS Word Mail Merge wizard.

   • Write a set of instructions for an inexperienced user that describes how to use the wizard.

   • Illustrate your instructions by setting up a mail merge in MS Word and taking screen shots (using Alt + PrtScr) as you work through the steps.

Graphics packages are a type of application software that can be used to create and manipulate images on a computer. The images produced using graphics packages can be used in many different ways such as:

- as a source of original artwork when using word processing, DTP or presentation software;
- to provide characters and backgrounds for computer games;
- to create graphics for use on websites;
- to provide special effects in feature films and TV programmes.

Graphics packages can be divided into two main groups – **painting packages** and **drawing packages**.

Painting packages

A **painting package** produces images by changing the colour of **pixels** on the screen, which are then coded as a pattern of bits to create a **bitmapped** graphics file. Bitmapped graphics are also used for pictures taken with a digital camera or scanned photographs.

The main advantage of using bitmapped graphics files is that individual pixels can be changed, which makes very detailed editing possible. This is particularly useful when photographs need to be changed in some way. **Photo editing packages** are often used for this; these are just a special type of painting package.

Figure 13.1 Serif PhotoPlus: a photo editing package

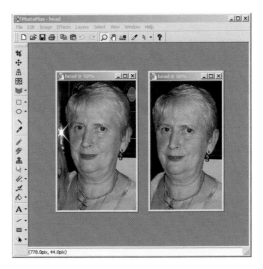

Figure 13.2 Photo editing packages are often used to remove unwanted elements in a photograph – can you spot the differences?

The main disadvantages of using bitmapped graphics files are:

- individual parts of an image cannot be resized – only the whole picture can be increased or decreased in size, which can create empty spaces, jagged edges or produce a blurred image;
- information has to be stored about every pixel in an image; this produces large files that use large amounts of backing storage space.

Figure 13.3 Resizing a bitmap can result in a blurred image

Examples of painting packages that can produce and manipulate bitmap images include MS Paint, PC Paintbrush, Adobe PhotoShop and JASC's Paint Shop Pro. These and other good painting packages share many common features.

Drawing packages

A **drawing package** produces images that are made up from a combination of lines and shapes such as circles, squares and rectangles. An image produced using a drawing package is saved as a **vector graphics file,** which contains a series of instructions that describe the individual lines and shapes making up the image.

Figure 13.4 Serif DrawPlus: a popular drawing package

The main advantages of using vector graphics files are:

- they take up much less storage space than bitmapped graphics files;
- each part of an image is treated as a separate object, which means that individual parts can be easily modified and resized if necessary.

The disadvantage of vector graphics is that they don't look as realistic as bitmapped graphics, which makes them unsuitable for storing and manipulating images like photographs.

Examples of drawing graphics packages include CorelDraw, Serif DrawPlus, MicroGraphix Designer and CAD (computer-aided design) packages such as AutoCAD. (CAD packages are explained in more detail later in Case Study 3.)

Features of drawing packages

Good drawing packages share many common features – some of these are described below.

- Tools to draw **straight lines** and **freehand lines**.
- Tools to draw regular **pre-defined shapes**, like rectangles and circles.

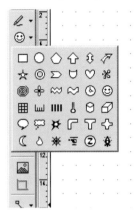

Figure 13.5 Pre-defined shape drawing tools

- A facility that allows text to be entered and the style and size of font changed.
- Tools to change, or **scale**, the size of objects.

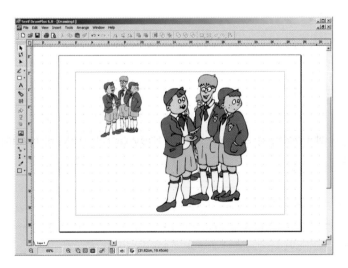

Figure 13.6 Changing, or scaling, the size of an object

- Tools to **rotate** objects.

Figure 13.7 Objects can be rotated in a circle either clockwise or anticlockwise by specifying the direction and angle of rotation

- Tools to **stretch** objects.

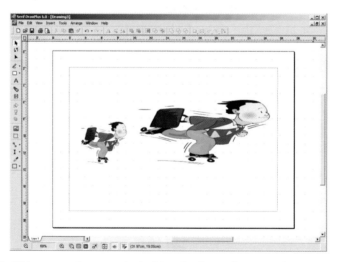

Figure 13.8 Objects can be stretched either horizontally or vertically, changing both their size and appearance

- Tools to **flip** objects either **horizontally** or **vertically** (or both!).

Figure 13.9 Flipping an object horizontally and vertically

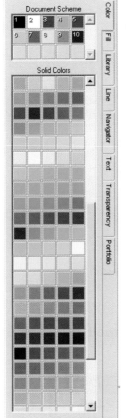

- A **paint palette** from which different colours and patterns can be chosen.

Figure 13.10 A paint palette

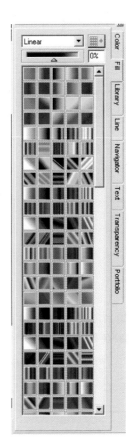

- A **fill** option for colouring in a shape or area on the screen with a colour or pattern from the paint palette

Figure 13.11 Some fill options

- A **clipart library** of pictures drawn by professional artists.
- A facility to **zoom** (or **magnify**) an area of the screen for more detailed editing.

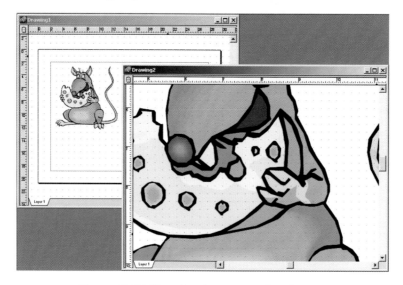

Figure 13.12 Zooming in on part of an image

- Tools to choose different types and sizes of **brush**.

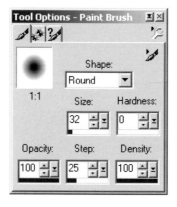

Figure 13.13 Special brushes such as an airbrush can be used to achieve different paint effects on the screen

In most graphics packages, features like these are chosen from a **toolbar** (or **tool palette**) where they are displayed as icons.

Figure 13.14 The toolbar of a graphics package

Exporting and importing graphics

If a picture produced using a graphics package is going to be used in another application, it may need to be saved in a special way. Different application packages don't necessarily understand each other's files. This special way of saving a file is called **exporting**. When an exported file is needed in another application, it needs to be opened in a special way as well. This process is called **importing**.

It is necessary to specify a **file format** when exporting and importing files. The format of a file determines exactly how the application will save it and, in the case of importing, what **graphics filter** to use to load a file in. The graphics filter 'translates' an exported file into a format that the application importing it can understand. There are many different graphics file formats, but most of them can be divided into two main groups: **vector format** and **bitmap format** files.

Vector format files are used by drawing packages and include:

.cgm	Computer Graphics Metafile
.wmf	Windows Metafile
.eps	Encapsulated Postscript

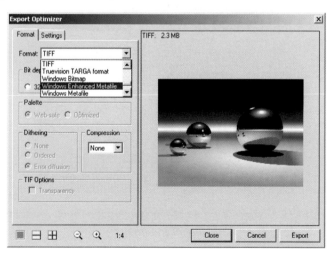

Figure 13.15 Exporting a graphic from a drawing package

Chapter 13

Bitmap format files are used by painting packages and include:

.bmp   Standard Bitmap File

.jpg   Joint Photographic Expert Group

.tif   Tagged Image File

.gif   Graphics Interchange File

.png   Portable Network Graphics

Standard bitmap format files tend to be quite large and take up a lot of disk space. This can be a problem if an image is being used, for example, on a Website where a large file would increase the download time for a web page. One way around this would be to convert the file to a different bitmap format which allows the file size to be reduced using compression. The main drawback of this technique is that the quality of the image is reduced each time the file is compressed further. JPG files support compression in this way, which makes them a very popular format.

Figure 13.16 Compressing a bitmap graphic too much reduces the quality of the image

GIF images are another popular bitmap format. They contain just 256 colours (compared with 16 million for JPG format) and are better for drawings and simple designs. This format is often used for logos and simple images on websites. Two useful features of GIF images are that they can be animated or have transparent backgrounds.

In the examination you could be asked to give or choose from a list some of the features that you would expect a typical graphics package to have.

Some possible answers are:

- *tools for drawing, e.g. pens, paintbrushes;*
- *a colour palette;*
- *a 'fill' tool;*
- *a set of pre-defined shapes;*
- *facilities to import and export graphics;*
- *tools to edit pictures or drawings;*
- *a tool for arranging objects in different 'layers';*
- *a 'zoom' tool for enlarging part of an image;*
- *tools for repositioning objects;*
- *tools for copying, cutting and pasting;*
- *tools for rotating objects;*
- *a facility to group and ungroup objects;*
- *a tool for erasing (or 'rubbing out') parts of a picture or drawing.*

TIP

Questions

1. Images produced using graphics packages can be either **bitmap** or **vector** format depending on the type of package used.

   (a) Explain what is meant by the term **bitmap format** and give one advantage offered by this type of graphic. (3)

   (b) Give **two** examples of bitmap format file types. (2)

   (c) Give **one** disadvantage of using bitmap format graphics. (1)

   (d) Explain what is meant by the term **vector format** and give one advantage offered by this type of graphic. (3)

   (e) Give **one** disadvantage of using vector format graphics. (1)

   (f) Give **two** examples of vector format file types. (2)

   (g) Give **one** disadvantage of using vector format graphics. (1)

2. A hotel has recently bought a **graphics package** which helps them design the layout of rooms for wedding receptions and other events.

   (a) Give **five features** (other than saving and printing) that you would expect the graphics package to contain. (5)

   (b) At the end of the design process for a wedding reception, the hotel printed out copies of the layout of the room. Give **three different** examples of people who would need a copy of the printout and give a reason why each would need it. (6)

   AQA (Short Course) 2002 Tier H

3. Explain why a **graphics filter** may be needed when importing a graphic into an application. (2)

4. A school secretary has used a painting package to improve the appearance of a photograph that will appear in the new school prospectus. The original and edited versions of the photograph are shown below.

   (a) Give **two input devices** that could have been used to capture the original image. (2)

   (b) Give **three** improvements the secretary has made to the **appearance** of the photograph by using editing tools in the painting package. (3)

   (c) For each improvement you have given in (b) above describe the editing tool the secretary has used. (3)

Web tasks

1. Visit the Free On-Line Dictionary of Computing (FOLDOC) at:
   http://wombat.doc.ic.ac.uk/foldoc/

   (a) Look up definitions of the keywords highlighted in this chapter.

   (b) Prepare a summary list of keywords and definitions to use for revision.

2. Visit the **About.com** website at:

   http://graphicssoft.about.com/library/weekly/aa000327a.htm

   - Read through the facts about vector and bitmap images;
   - Prepare a summary fact sheet for each type of graphic.

3. Visit the **About.com** website at:

   http://graphicssoft.about.com/library/extra/blhangman1.htm

   Test your knowledge of graphics software terminology by playing the hangman game.

4. Find out how computer graphics are used to generate TV and film special effects at:

   http://library.thinkquest.org/3496/nfwelcome.html

   - Choose and read through one of the topics of discussion.
   - Prepare a summary presentation for the rest of your group to report back what you find out.

Desk top publishing, or **DTP** for short, is the use of a **desk top publishing package** on a computer to produce publications such as newsletters, magazines, leaflets, posters, and books. The DTP process is mainly concerned with organising the layout and appearance of text and graphics in a publication. The contents of the publication should already have been prepared using a word processing package for text, and graphics packages for pictures, diagrams and illustrations.

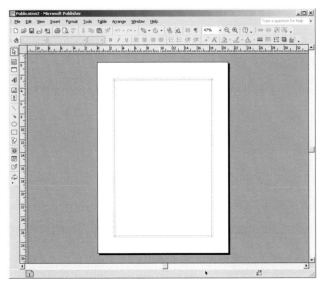

Figure 14.1 MS Publisher: a popular DTP package

Desk top publishing hardware

To work efficiently with DTP software, a high-specification computer with a large amount of RAM and a fast processor is required. This is so that changes can be made to a publication and their effect seen straight away, without having to wait for the computer to deal with the many thousands of instructions and calculations that this type of work generates.

The files produced using DTP software contain both graphics and text and can be quite large, so a high-capacity hard disk drive is needed to store them. It is also a good idea for a DTP system to have a Zip drive or CD-writer, to allow large files to be more easily transferred between computers.

DTP software displays publications in **WYSIWYG** format – which stands for "What you see is what you get". A high-resolution monitor with a large screen is best for this application, so that you can actually see what you're getting without straining your eyes.

Another essential piece of hardware for any DTP system is a scanner, which is used to import any hand-drawn or printed graphics into a publication. To ensure that finished publications are of a high standard, the scanner should be able to scan high-resolution images.

To output completed publications, a high-quality printer, such as a laser printer or high-specification inkjet printer, is needed. A colour laser printer will give the best quality output but is also the most expensive option.

Features of desk top publishing packages

Some of the most important features that any good desk top publishing package should offer are:

Frames

Most DTP packages are frame-based – this means that text and graphics are placed inside rectangular boxes called frames. The main advantage offered by frames is that they can be arranged in layers on top of each other. This can be useful if, for example, some text needs to be placed over a graphic.

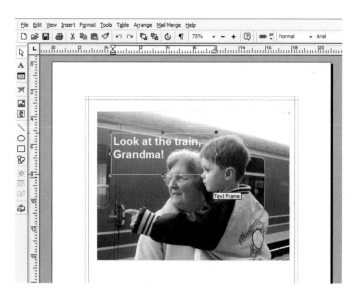

Figure 14.2 Placing a text frame over a picture frame in MS Publisher

163

Design wizards

Design wizards are provided to give step-by-step help when creating common types of publication such as newspapers, newsletters, flyers and greetings cards.

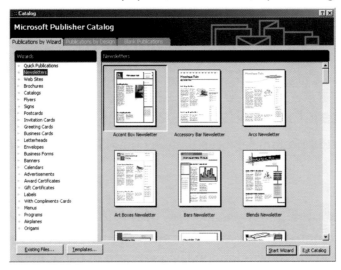

Figure 14.3 Some of the design wizards offered by MS Publisher

Fonts

A good DTP package will include a large variety of fonts, which can be resized however the user requires.

Styles

Styles allow the user to define the font style, size and colour of text. Once a style has been defined, it can be applied to any part of the text whenever necessary. This saves time when text is being formatted and helps to keep its appearance consistent throughout a publication.

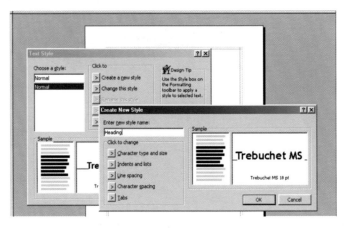

Figure 14.4 Defining styles in MS Publisher

Borders

Borders can be used to make objects stand out – this may just be a coloured line, or something more sophisticated.

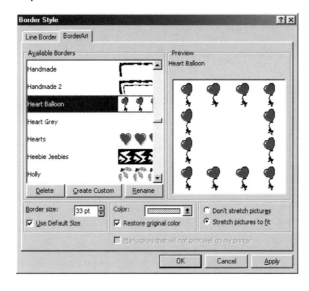

Figure 14.5 Border styles in MS Publisher

Colour

A good DTP package will include a large choice of colours, which can be used to fill in areas of a page or make text, borders and lines stand out more. Various tints, shades and patterns of colour are usually offered, along with the facility to create a customised colour scheme for a publication.

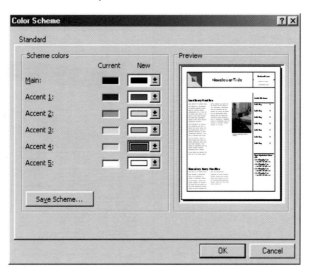

Figure 14.6 Creating a customised colour scheme in MS Publisher

Clipart

DTP packages often have a library of artwork supplied with them from which graphics can be copied and pasted into a publication.

Character and line spacing

The spacing between characters can be adjusted by using a feature called **kerning**. All DTP packages offer this facility, along with options to shrink and stretch text.

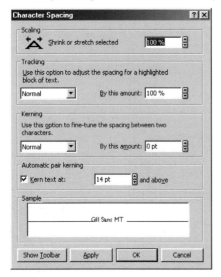

Figure 14.7 Adjusting character spacing in MS publisher

The spacing between lines can be changed by adjusting the **leading** (this was explained in the last chapter).

Text columns

DTP packages all offer a facility which allows the user to set up the pages of a publication to have a certain number of text columns. This is useful when producing a newsletter or newspaper.

Figure 14.8 Text columns in a newsletter style page layout

The stages of desk top publishing

The process of using a desk top publishing package to produce publications can be broken down into a series of stages:

1. The contents of the publication are prepared first; this will involve some or possibly all of the following activities:

   - using a word processing package to prepare text and check for mistakes with the spell and grammar check facilities;

   - capturing images using a scanner or digital camera;

   - finding appropriate images in clipart libraries on CD-ROM;

   - finding and downloading appropriate images from the Internet;

   - creating graphs or charts to represent information stored in a spreadsheet or database;

   - using graphics packages to prepare captured images or create new illustrations.

2. The general layout of the pages is designed and **page templates** are created. A template defines the standard layout for a page, such as how many columns of text are needed and where spaces must be left for graphics. Once a template has been set up it can be used to create as many individual pages as required, each with the same basic layout. This greatly reduces the time that it takes to organise the layout of each page.

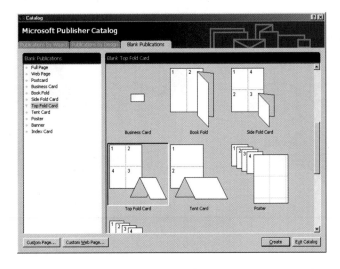

Figure 14.9 Some of the blank page templates available in MS Publisher

3. Text and graphics are imported and put into place on the pages.

Text and graphics are normally placed in frames. Text frames can have their size adjusted or be linked together if text doesn't fit.

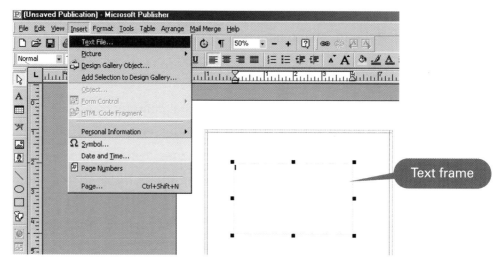

Figure 14.10 Inserting a text frame

Graphics that don't fit inside a frame must have their size altered by cropping or scaling.

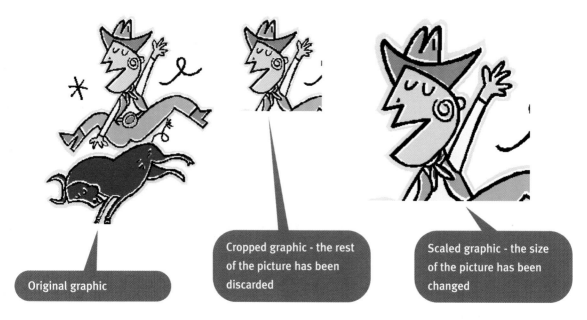

Figure 14.11 Cropping and scaling a graphic

Where text overlaps a graphic it can be flowed or wrapped around the graphic.

Figure 14.12 Wrapping text around a graphic

4. Once the layout has been finalised, the completed publication is printed and 'proof read' to check for any errors. Any necessary corrections or changes to the layout can then be made. After this, a final high-quality 'master copy' can be printed using a laser printer. This master copy can be used to make further copies on a photocopying machine. Alternatively, the file can be sent to a professional printing company, using e-mail (or through the conventional post by saving it on disk).

Desk top publishing packages offer many features that can be used to improve the appearance of printed publications. You could be asked to give some of these features in the examination and explain how they could be used to improve a sample publication.

Some of the more common features you might include in your answer are:

* *frames to produce a wide variety of professional layouts;*
* *the facility to easily change font size to make text more interesting and easy to read;*
* *the facility to easily change font style to make text more attractive;*
* *the facility to change, add and position graphics easily to make a publication more interesting and appealing;*
* *colour and shading facilities;*
* *a wide variety of border options;*
* *design wizards.*

TIP

Questions

1. A group of young people at a local tennis club are going to use a DTP (Desk Top Publishing) package to produce a notice to advertise a tennis summer school. Their first attempt is shown here.

> Tennis Summer School
>
> Dates – August 4th to August 7th
>
> Time – 10am to 3pm
>
> Chief Coach – Mrs Perry
>
> Clothing – suitable tennis clothing must be worn
>
> Cost - £20 to members, £30 to non-members
>
> This course is open to all age groups – come along and have fun.

They were not very pleased with their first attempt and they have used the DTP (Desk Top Publishing) package to make a number of changes. Their new poster is shown below.

> # **Tennis Summer School**
>
> **Dates** – August 4th to August 7th
>
> **Time** – 10am to 3pm
>
> **Chief Coach** – Mrs Perry
>
> **Clothing** – suitable tennis clothing must be worn
>
> **Cost** - £20 to members, £30 to non-members
>
> This course is open to all age groups – come along and have fun.

(a) Give **four** features of the DTP (Desk Top Publishing) package that have been used to produce the changes to the new poster. (4)

(b) Describe **three different** features of the DTP (Desk Top Publishing) package that could be used to improve the poster. Give a reason why each feature might be used. (6)

AQA (NEAB) 2000 Paper 1 Tier F

2. A video shop used a DTP (Desk Top Publishing) package to change **Flyer A** into **Flyer B**.

Flyer A

Vic's Videos

Special Offers

Hire two videos and get a third video free.

Pay for a one-night hire and keep the video for 2 nights.

Hire three videos and get a large drink and large popcorn free.

Don't delay
Hire today

Flyer B

Vic's Videos

Special Offers

• Hire two videos and get a third video free.

• Pay for a one-night hire and keep the video for 2 nights.

• Hire three videos and get a large drink and large popcorn free.

Don't delay
Hire today

(a) Give **five** changes that have been made to **Flyer A**. (5)

(b) Give **two other** changes that could have been made to the presentation of **Flyer A** using a DTP package. (2)

AQA 2003 Foundation Tier

3. A small chain of video rental shops wants to use a software package to improve its advertising materials which give details of branch addresses, opening times and the services they offer.

(a) Give the best type of **application software** to use to improve the advertising materials. (1)

(b) Give **three** features typically offered by this type of software that make it suitable for this type of task. (3)

(c) Give **one** example of how **each feature listed in part (b) above** could be used to improve the advertising materials. (3)

Web tasks

1. Visit the Free On-Line Dictionary of Computing (FOLDOC) at:
    http://wombat.doc.ic.ac.uk/foldoc/

    (a) Look up definitions of the key words highlighted in this chapter.

    (b) Prepare a summary list of keywords and definitions to use
    for revision.

2. Visit the **About.com** website at:

    http://desktoppub.about.com/library/weekly/blquiz_basicsintro.htm

    Test your knowledge of Desk Top Publishing by working through the quiz.

6. Visit the **About.com** website at:

    http://desktoppub.about.com/cs/designguidelines/tp/designdisasters.htm

    • Read through the top five design disasters to avoid.

    • Prepare a summary sheet of the key points, to help someone
    new to using DTP software to produce good quality results.

7. Read reviews of popular DTP packages at:

    www.itreviews.co.uk/software/s119.htm

    Carry out some more research on these packages before preparing a
    guide for an inexperienced computer user to help them choose the right
    DTP package.

The **World Wide Web**, or **WWW** for short, is the largest part of the Internet. It is a body of information that spans the entire Internet. Individuals and organisations provide pages of information on **websites**, which begin at their **home page**. Web pages are created using **Hypertext Mark-up Language (HTML)**. This is a fairly simple computer programming language which tells **web browsers** like MS Internet Explorer how to display information. Computer users who have no knowledge of HTML can use **web design packages** to produce individual web pages or complete websites in a WYSIWYG environment, very similar to that offered by word processing and DTP software to produce printed publications. This chapter describes the features offered by typical web design packages such as MS FrontPage or Macromedia Dreamweaver.

Hyperlinks

Hyperlinks are used to navigate around a website. A hyperlink is a piece of text or a graphic that contains the address of another location on the Web. When a user clicks on a hyperlink, they are taken to the location specified in its address. A text hyperlink is normally identified by a distinctive colour, which changes after it has been clicked.

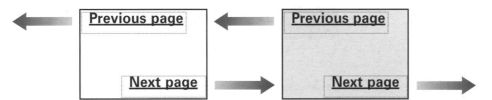

Figure 15.1 Hyperlinks are used in a website to move between pages or to other websites

The facility to create text or graphical hyperlinks is a basic feature of any web design package. Without this there would be no way of linking different pages or sections of hypertext together so that users could move around easily within a website.

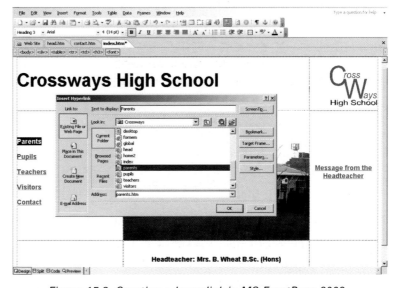

Figure 15.2 Creating a hyperlink in MS FrontPage 2003

173

Hot spots

A **hot spot** is an area on an object that contains a hyperlink. An image can contain a single hot spot, or multiple hot spots. When a user clicks on a hot spot, they are taken to the location specified in its hyperlink. To create a hot spot, an active area must be defined on an image and a hyperlink associated with it.

Figure 15.3 Creating a hot spot. A hyperlink is created and associated with an active area defined by a shape such as a rectangle or circle

TIP *In the examination you could be asked to explain what is meant by the terms* **hyperlink** *and* **hot spot**. *Make sure that you can explain what each of these terms means.*

Tables

Ordinary HTML code can place objects only on the left, right or centre of a page. Most web designers get around this problem by basing their page layout designs around **tables**. Objects are positioned on the web page by placing them inside individual cells in a table. This helps in the creation of more interesting page layouts by allowing text and graphics to be arranged easily.

A good web design package will allow tables to be created and manipulated by:

• resizing individual cells or groups of cells;
• merging cells;

- inserting or deleting cells, rows and columns;
- aligning text or other objects within cells;
- filling cells with colours, patterns or graphics;
- using line and border styles around cells.

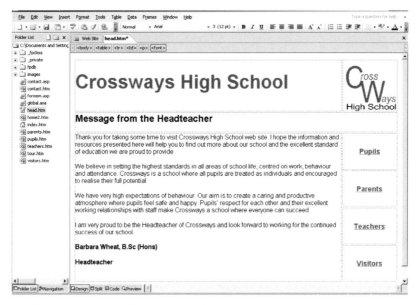

Figure 15.4a A table has been used in a web design package to organise the text on a web page into a table of contents containing hyperlinks to other pages. This is a common use of tables on web pages

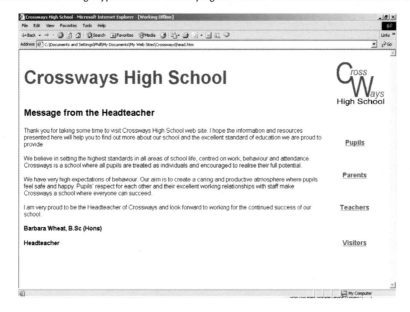

Figure 15.4b The table cannot be seen on the finished web page

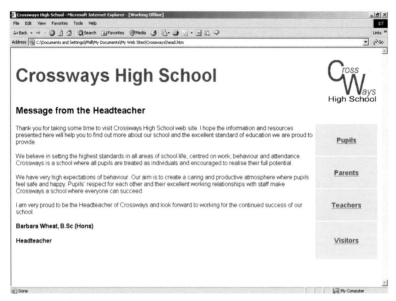

Figure 15.4c Individual cells or groups of cells in tables can have coloured backgrounds and borders

Importing text and graphics

A good web design package will allow text and graphics to be imported, placed on a page and manipulated. Some packages offer more advanced features which allow text or graphics to be animated. Possible sources of images could be clipart on CD-ROM, scanned images, pictures from a digital camera, or graphics from other Websites. Text could be from a file created with a word processing application.

Page navigation

It is important that the structure of a Website can be changed, so that its pages can be organised into a logical order which users can easily navigate their way around. A good web design package will allow the overall structure of a Website to be viewed, and the order of pages to be changed without disrupting the hyperlinks between them.

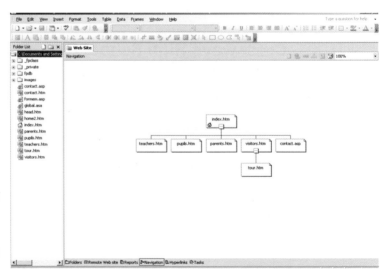

Figure 15.5 In MS FrontPage and other web design packages the structure of a website is displayed as a tree. To change the position of a page it can be 'dragged and dropped' to a new location in the tree

Good web design

The use of a good web design package won't necessarily result in the production of a well-designed web page. The identity of the target audience, contents and overall layout are important factors to consider when planning a Website. Some basic rules that should be followed during the design process are:

* write clearly and be brief;
* don't overcrowd pages with large amounts of text and graphics;
* don't use a lot of graphics – this can make pages take a long time to load;
* put the most important items at the top of a page – this will attract attention and make people want to look at the rest of the page;
* use headings and lists to summarise topics so that readers can scan the contents of pages quickly;
* use bold and italic text to attract attention, rather than special effects such as animated or flashing text, which can be annoying;
* try to make your site easy to navigate by using frames or putting a table of contents at the beginning of a section.

In the examination you could be asked to give or choose from a list some of the features that you would expect a typical web design package to have.

Some possible answers are:

* *facilities that allow text and pictures to be imported;*
* *tools to create and manipulate tables to position objects like text and graphics;*
* *tools to create hyperlinks from text and graphics;*
* *tools to create hot spots over parts of pictures.*

TIP

Questions

1. Explain what is meant by the following terms.

    (a) World Wide Web   (1)

    (b) Home page   (1)

    (c) HTML   (2)

    (d) Hyperlink   (2)

    (e) Hotspot   (2)

2. You have been asked to produce some web pages for the school Website.

    (a) Give **four** features of a web design package that would make this task easier than writing the necessary HTML code directly.   (4)

    (b) Name and give a reason for **three** factors you would need to take into account when designing the web pages.   (6)

3. One of your friends is considering buying a web design package for their PC. Describe **five** essential features that a good web design package should include. Your description must explain how each feature can help users to produce well-designed web pages.   (10)

Web tasks

1. Visit the Free On-Line Dictionary of computing (FOLDOC) at:
    http://wombat.doc.ic.ac.uk/foldoc/

    (a) Look up definitions of the keywords highlighted in this chapter.

    (b) Prepare a summary list of keywords and definitions to use for revision.

2. Visit **www.useit.com/alertbox/991003.html**

    (a) Read through the 'ten good deeds in web design'.

    (b) When you've finished visit
    http://itserver.footscray.vic.edu.au/it/webdesign/quiz.htm and
    take the web design quiz.

3. Visit **http://webreference.com/greatsite.HTML**

    (a) Read the advice on 'what makes a great website'.

    (b) Prepare a summary of the information there for someone new to designing and building Websites.

4. Read reviews of popular web design packages at:

    www.webwizguide.info/software/default.asp

    Carry out some more research on these packages before preparing a guide for an inexperienced computer user to help them choose a package.

Computer models are used to predict and investigate how a device or process might behave given a certain set of conditions. Some of the more common uses for computer models are:

- car manufacturers use models to test the effects of crashes on new cars, which is a lot more cost effective than building and crashing real cars;

- civil engineers use models to predict the effects of natural hazards such as strong winds or earthquakes on designs for new buildings and bridges;

- aircraft manufacturers use models to test the aerodynamics of new designs and avoid the expense of building real prototypes;

- the UK Treasury uses a complicated financial model to investigate the possible effects of changes to public spending, interest rates or taxes on the economy;

- many businesses use financial models to investigate ways of cutting costs and improving profitability;

- weather forecasting services use very complicated models of the atmosphere to predict how the weather will behave;

- scientists use computer models to investigate the effects of changes to the climate brought about by global warming.

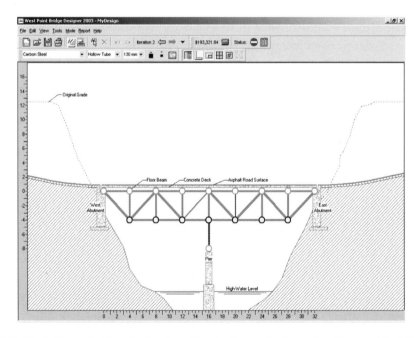

Figure 16.1 Modelling a bridge design to estimate the cost of construction and test its strength

Building models

Computer models exist only inside the computer as a program that contains a set of **rules** expressed as mathematical equations – they do not take up space in the outside world. The rules of a model describe an object or process and the **variables** that can be changed to affect the way that it behaves. It is this set of rules that determines how good a model is – incomplete or poorly expressed rules will make inaccurate and unreliable predictions.

Computer models can be built in a number of different ways. Spreadsheet packages are often used to construct models, particularly for situations where the finances of a project need to be investigated before deciding how to proceed.

Animal	Cost per week to feed each animal	Number of animals	Total cost per week	Total cost per year	Number of adoption shares	Number of adoption shares sold	Value of adoption shares sold	Money still needed
Buffalo	£12	15	£180	£9,360	312	80	£2,400	£6,960
Chimpanzee	£12	7	£84	£4,368	146	122	£3,660	£708
Crocodile	£5	8	£40	£2,080	69	12	£360	£1,720
Deer	£7	12	£84	£4,368	146	18	£540	£3,828
Elephant	£46	8	£368	£19,136	638	89	£2,670	£16,466
Giraffe	£12	4	£48	£2,496	83	52	£1,560	£936
Kangaroo	£5	7	£35	£1,820	61	45	£1,350	£470
Lion	£12	8	£96	£4,992	166	132	£3,960	£1,032
Parrot	£1	6	£6	£312	10	3	£90	£222
Penguin	£5	22	£110	£5,720	191	109	£3,270	£2,450
Python	£1	5	£5	£260	9	3	£90	£170
Sea Lion	£23	10	£230	£11,960	399	212	£6,360	£5,600
Tiger	£23	5	£115	£5,980	199	182	£5,460	£520
Wolf	£3	5	£15	£780	26	9	£270	£510
Zebra	£12	7	£84	£4,368	146	62	£1,860	£2,508
	Total food bill			£78,000		Total still needed		£44,100

Figure 16.2 A spreadsheet used to model the finances of running an animal adoption scheme in a zoo

To build more complex models special programming languages can be used – SIMSCRIPT and SIMULA are examples of such languages. Another alternative is to use an application package specially designed for building models. Modus Model Builder is an example of such a package and is sometimes used in schools to teach students how to use and build computer models.

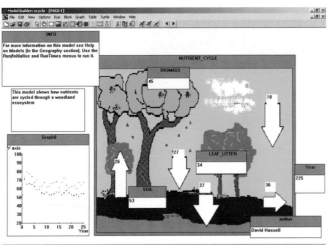

Figure 16.3 This model, created using Modus Model Builder, shows how nutrients are cycled through a woodland ecosystem

181

Simulations

A computer simulation is a special type of computer model which recreates a real system from outside the computer. Simulations are often used to train people how to deal with situations that are too difficult, expensive or dangerous to recreate and practise for real. Many computer games are simulations of real-life situations such as driving a racing car, flying a jet fighter, or playing in a premiership football match.

A good example of a simulation is a flight simulator, which is used to train pilots how to deal with situations that would be expensive and dangerous to practise using a real aircraft. A flight simulator consists of a working replica of the flight deck of an aeroplane, mounted on hydraulic supports that are used to create a realistic feeling of movement. Simulation software provides a view of the simulated outside world through the cockpit window, controls the instrument readings and responds to commands given by the pilot.

The main advantage of using a flight simulator is that pilots can learn how to deal with dangerous situations without putting lives at risk or damaging expensive equipment.

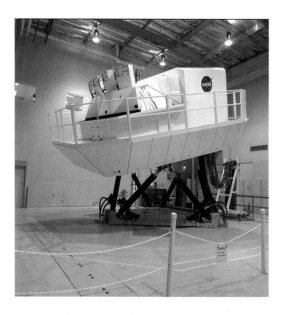

Figure 16.4 NASA's Boeing 747 flight simulator

Figure 16.5 Inside the cockpit of NASA's Boeing 747 flight simulator

Using computer models and simulations to predict and investigate how devices or processes might behave in different conditions has both advantages and disadvantages. You could be asked to give or choose some of these in the examination.

For the advantages some possible answers are:

* *expensive prototypes or full-size mock-ups don't need to be built;*
* *no equipment is damaged;*
* *people are not put in any danger;*
* *modifications can be made easily and re-tested quickly.*

For the disadvantages some possible answers are:

* *the results depend on how good the model is – a poor model will give unreliable results;*
* *simulations can't completely recreate the pressures that a person might be under in a real-life situation.*

TIP

Questions

1. Computer models are used to predict and investigate how devices or processes might behave in different conditions.

    (a) Explain why it is important to consider carefully the rules and **variables** that are needed when a new model is being developed. (2)

    (b) Give **two** examples of situations where computer models are used. (2)

    (c) For each situation you have given in (b) above explain how the computer model would be used. (2)

2. A school's network manager has been asked by the Headteacher to investigate the costs involved in upgrading a computer room. The network manager has set up the simple spreadsheet model shown below to help with this task.

	A	B	C	D	E
1	**Room 58 upgrade costs**				
2					
3	**Item**	**Unit cost**	**Number needed**	**Total cost per item**	
4	Mini tower PC base unit	£399.00	20	£7,980.00	
5	14" TFT Monitor	£249.00	20	£4,980.00	
6	Mouse	£1.95	20	£39.00	
7	Keyboard	£4.99	20	£99.80	
8	Headphones	£3.95	20	£79.00	
9	MS Windows Licence	£68.00	20	£1,360.00	
10	MS Office Licence	£74.00	20	£1,480.00	
11	Scanner	£45.00	4	£180.00	
12	Data projector	£1,995.00	1	£1,995.00	
13	Interactive whiteboard	£1,650.00	1	£1,650.00	
14					
15			**Total cost**	£19,842.80	
16					

    (a) Give **one data format** that has been used on the spreadsheet. (1)

    (b) Describe **two** ways that **cell formatting** has been used to change the appearance of the spreadsheet. (4)

    (c) Give **three** cells that contain **variables**. (3)

    (d) Give **two** cells that contain **rules**. (2)

    (e) Explain how the network manager could use the spreadsheet to prepare a set of different cost options for the Headteacher. (3)

3. Firefighters use simulators to gain experience of driving their fire engines at high speeds.

    (a) Give **two** reasons why a simulator would be used to gain experience of high speed driving rather than driving on the road. (2)

    (b) All simulators rely on rules built into the controlling software. Which **three** of the following are rules that could reasonably be built into this driving simulation?

	Tick **three** boxes only
It takes longer to stop on wet roads rather than dry roads	
All motorway driving must be fast	
Fire engines must have a safety check every month	
How visibility will change in foggy conditions	
The maximum speed of the fire engine	
The telephone number of the local police	

(3)

    (c) Name **two other** situations (other than driving) in which computer simulation might reasonably be used. (2)

AQA (Short Course) 2003

4. Simulators can be used to gain experience of flying aircraft.

    (a) Give **one** example of people who may need to use such a simulator as part of their job. (1)

    (b) Give **two** reasons why a simulator would be used in this situation. (2)

5. Computer simulations are often used to train people how to do jobs that might be dangerous in real life.

    (a) Which **three** of the following are advantages of using computer simulations to train people?

	Tick **three** boxes only
full size mock-ups don't need to be built	
people can be trained in much less time	
computer simulations are cheaper	
no equipment is damaged	
more people can be trained	
people are not put in any danger	

(3)

    (b) Name **three** jobs where computer simulation might be used to train people. (2)

Web tasks

1. Visit the Free On-Line Dictionary of Computing (FOLDOC) at:
    http://wombat.doc.ic.ac.uk/foldoc/

    (a) Look up definitions of the keywords highlighted in this chapter.

    (b) Prepare a summary list of keywords and definitions to use for revision.

2. Visit **www.si.umich.edu/~pne/modeling.world.htm#Heading2**

    Read this article by Professor Paul Edwards of the University of Michigan School of Information, which describes some of the early uses of computer models and simulations.

3. The UCLA Department of Architecture and Urban Design (AUD) is building a real-time simulation model of the city of Los Angeles.

    Check this out at:
    www.ust.ucla.edu/ustweb/projects.html

4. Use the West Point Bridge Designer software to hold a class challenge to see who can come up with the strongest, cheapest bridge design.

    Note: Your teacher will need to make sure that the software has been downloaded from **http://bridgecontest.usma.edu/** and installed on the school network before you can attempt this task.

5. Prepare a presentation on the history and uses of flight simulators.

    You can start by carrying out some research at these sites:

    www.fact-index.com/f/fl/flight_simulator.html
    www.yorkshireflightcentre.co.uk/about-simulators.php
    www.southwest.com/careers/training_facility.html
    www.csa.cz/en/aktivity/posadky/pos_pilot.htm

Computer control is the use of a computer to monitor and control an external process. **Input sensors** are connected to the computer, and are used to monitor the various parts of a process that it is controlling. Sensors are used to measure changes in the value of some **physical quantity**, such as temperature or light.

Input signals are useless to the computer if it does not know how to interpret them or what actions to take as a result. Before any process can be controlled by a computer, a **control program** must be written by a human to tell the computer what to do.

The signals from input sensors are used by the computer to monitor what is going on in the process that it is controlling. Depending upon the value of an input signal from a sensor and the instructions given in its control program, the computer makes a decision about whether an output signal is needed, to switch on or off some part of the process's hardware.

Digital and analogue signals

There are two types of input signal which a sensor can send to a computer: **digital** and **analogue**. The simplest computer control systems are those which use digital signals. This is because digital signals are easier to process as they can have only two possible values: **on** (or **true**) and **off** (or **false**). An example of a sensor which sends out a digital signal is an **infra-red sensor**. These are most commonly used by computer-controlled burglar alarms. Infra-red sensors send out an invisible beam of light, which is 'broken' when something moves through it. Breaking the beam causes the sensor to send out an 'on' signal to the computer. These digital signals are simple to process because they can be sent directly to the computer, which is itself a digital device.

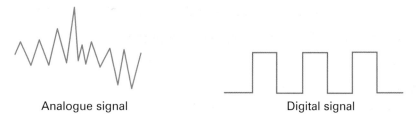

Analogue signal   Digital signal

Figure 17.1 Digital signals can have only two possible values: on or off

Analogue signals are different because they can have any value. A **temperature sensor** is an example of a sensor which sends out analogue signals. Temperature is a physical quantity which can have any number of different values over a given period of time.

To be able to process analogue signals sent to it by a sensor, the computer needs an **analogue-to-digital converter (ADC)** or other similar type of **interface** connected to one of its **input ports**. These devices convert the sensor's **analogue signal**, which the computer can't process directly, into an equivalent **digital signal**, which the computer *can* process directly.

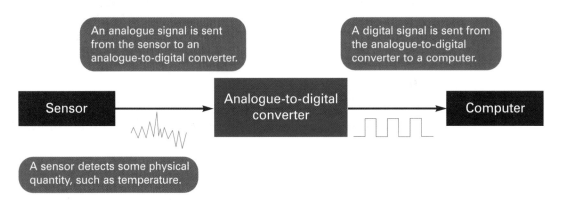

Figure 17.2 Using an analogue-to-digital converter in a control system

Feedback control systems

Feedback control systems use the values of their output signals to affect the values of their input signals. Feedback is useful when a certain set of conditions needs to be constantly maintained. Suppose, for example, that you wanted to use computer control to keep the temperature in your bedroom between 21°C and 25°C and you have a heat lamp and a cooling fan connected to your computer. If the temperature was less than 21°C the computer would send a signal to the heat lamp to turn it on. The computer would keep checking the temperature, and once it was greater than or equal to 21°C the computer would send a signal to the heat lamp to turn it off. If the temperature was more than 25°C, the computer would send a signal to the cooling fan to turn it on. The computer would keep checking the temperature, and once it was less than or equal to 25°C the computer would send a signal to the cooling fan to turn it off. If the temperature was between 21°C and 25°C the computer would do nothing. This system is using feedback because it is using its output signals to make changes to the conditions outside, which will affect its input signals.

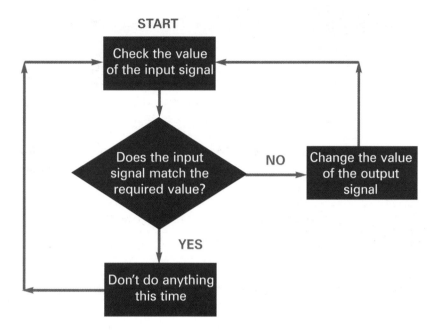

Figure 17.3 Flowchart for a feedback control system

Sensors

The types of sensor used by a computer-controlled system depend upon what sort of process is being controlled. There are many different types of sensor which can each measure some physical quantity outside the computer. Temperature, pressure, light, water and moisture levels, relative humidity, movement and wind speed are just some examples of the physical quantities that sensors can detect. The data that the sensors detect is in the form of analogue data, which is converted to digital data before it is sent to the computer. Some common examples of computer-controlled systems and the different types of sensors used by them are described below.

Many computer-controlled robots use a **bump sensor** to detect when they have struck another object. This can be used to help a robot 'feel' its way around things.

Computer-controlled greenhouses use **moisture sensors** to detect if the soil is becoming too wet or too dry, and **temperature sensors** to detect if the air is too warm or too cold. Some greenhouses also use light sensors to detect if the amount of light during the day falls to a point where it becomes too dark.

Figure 17.4 Industrial greenhouses use computer control systems

Traffic lights have sensors to detect traffic. One type of sensor used by traffic lights is a loop of wire buried in the approach road to the lights. This sensor detects the movement of cars on the road. Another type of sensor that detects the approach of vehicles is mounted on top of the traffic lights and looks like a small camera. This sensor is actually very similar to the infra-red movement detector used by a burglar alarm.

Figure 17.5 Sensors are buried in the road or mounted on top of traffic lights to detect approaching vehicles

Burglar alarm systems use **passive infra-red** sensors, or **PIRs** for short, to detect movement in a room. **Magnetic catches** can also be used to detect the opening of a door or window.

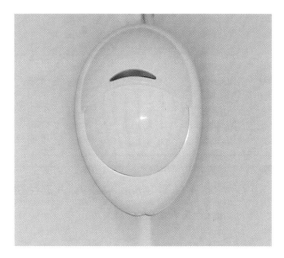

Figure 17.6 PIR sensors are used in home burglar alarm systems

In the examination you could be asked to give or choose suitable sensors for a control system. You could also be asked to explain how a control system works.

TIP

Actuators

A computer-controlled system would be useless if it could use sensors to detect what was going on in the outside world but do nothing about it. As we have already seen, computers can send out signals to turn on or off devices like heaters and lights so that they can affect what is going on in the outside world. Many control systems need to control devices that can move, such as a motor in a greenhouse to open or close a window. A device called an **actuator** is used to generate signals that can make devices move. Signals are sent from computers to actuators to control the movement of things like hydraulic, pneumatic or motorised systems.

LOGO

LOGO is a computer programming language that is often used in education to teach students about computer control. LOGO instructions are used to control the movement of a small shape, called a **turtle**, around the screen.

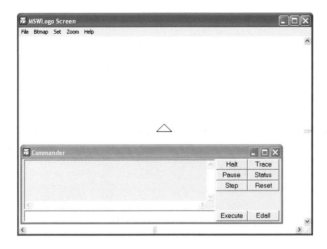

Figure 17.7 MSW Logo: a popular version of LOGO

LOGO commands

To make the turtle move on the screen, the following commands are used:

FORWARD

This command moves the turtle forward by a number of steps specified by the user. So, for example, to move the turtle 30 steps forward on the screen the instruction **FORWARD 30** would be used.

Figure 17.8 Moving
the turtle forward

RIGHT

This command turns the turtle to the right by an angle measured in degrees specified by the user. So, for example, to move the turtle to the right by an angle of 90° the command **RIGHT 90** would be used.

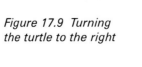

Figure 17.9 Turning
the turtle to the right

LEFT

This command turns the turtle to the left by an angle measured in degrees specified by the user. So, for example, to move the turtle to the left by an angle of 45° the command **LEFT 45** would be used.

BACKWARD

This command moves the turtle back by a number of steps specified by the user. So, for example, to move the turtle 40 steps back on the screen the instruction **BACKWARD 40** would be used.

PENUP

This command lifts the pen up and stops the turtle from drawing as it moves along.

PENDOWN

This puts the pen back down if it has been lifted up, so that the turtle will start drawing again as it moves along.

CLEARSCREEN

This command clears the screen, wiping everything that the turtle has drawn.

LOGO commands can be typed in one line at a time by the user. So, for example, if the user wanted to draw a square with sides 40 steps long they would need to type in the following instructions one line at a time:

> **FORWARD 40**
>
> **RIGHT 90**
>
> **FORWARD 40**
>
> **RIGHT 90**
>
> **FORWARD 40**
>
> **RIGHT 90**
>
> **FORWARD 40**

A quicker way to do this would be to use the **REPEAT** command, so the user could type:

> **REPEAT 4 [FORWARD 40 RIGHT 90]**

This command would repeat the instructions inside the square brackets four times to build up the sides of the square.

To draw the square without having to type in the same instructions over and over again, a **procedure** must be defined. This means that the set of instructions that draw the square are typed in and given a name. Once this has been done, the user can tell LOGO to draw the square by typing in just the name of the procedure. To define a procedure to draw the square, the user would type in the following commands:

> **TO SQUARE**
>
> **REPEAT 4[FORWARD 40 RIGHT 90]**
>
> **END**

All that the user would have to do to draw the square now would be to simply type the word **SQUARE**. This word could even be used in other instructions or procedures.

TIP

In the examination you could be given a set of commands similar to those used by LOGO and asked to draw the shape that would be produced if they were followed. When answering this type of question, work carefully through the commands ticking off each one as you carry it out. Marks are often lost when commands are missed out (causing a completely different shape to be drawn)!

Microprocessors

A **microprocessor** is basically just another name for a CPU. Microprocessors are used to control **automatic machines**. A washing machine is an example of an automatic machine. It is able to follow different wash programs by following pre-programmed sets of instructions, called **control programs**, that are stored inside its microprocessor. Automatic machines don't need to be supervised, because they are operated by a microprocessor following a control program. Microprocessors can be found around the home inside everyday electrical devices like video recorders, camcorders, hi-fi systems, microwave ovens, dishwashers and burglar alarms.

Figure 17.10 Everyday household appliances like washing machines use microprocessors

Questions

1. Give **one** suitable type of sensor for each of the computer control applications listed below. In each case give one reason for your choice of sensor.

   (a) Turning a security light on at dusk.

   (b) Stopping a factory robot from bumping into things.

   (c) Checking if plants need watering in a greenhouse.

   (d) Detecting the traffic approaching a pedestrian crossing.

   (e) Monitoring a baby's temperature in an incubator.

   (f) Detecting movement in a house for a burglar alarm.   (12)

2. A computer system controls a robot turtle. At the front, the turtle holds a pen. When the turtle moves, the pen leaves a line on the paper beneath it.
   The turtle is moved by typing commands into the computer system.
   The commands which are used to move the turtle are as follows:

   PENUP

   PENDOWN

   FORWARD distance   (in units)

   BACKWARD distance   (in units)

   RIGHT angle   (in degrees)

PENUP would lift the pen up from the paper. No line would be drawn until there is a PENDOWN command.

PENDOWN would put the pen down onto the paper and a line would be drawn until there is a PENUP command.

FORWARD 5 would move the turtle forward 5 units.

BACKWARD 5 would move the turtle backward 5 units.

RIGHT 45 would turn the turtle right through an angle of 45 degrees.

On the grid on the next page, **draw the shape** that would be produced if the following commands were followed.

PENDOWN
FORWARD 5
RIGHT 90
FORWARD 2
RIGHT 90
FORWARD 5
RIGHT 90
FORWARD 2
PENUP
BACKWARD 7
PENDOWN
FORWARD 4
RIGHT 90
FORWARD 1
RIGHT 90
FORWARD 4   Starting
RIGHT 90   position
FORWARD 1

(7)

AQA (NEAB) 2002 (Short Course) Tier F

3.   (a) Explain what is meant by the term **microprocessor**.   (2)

(a) Give **four** different types of household device that are controlled by microprocessors.   (4)

(b) For each device given in part (b) above give **one** example of what the microprocessor would control.   (4)

4. A garden centre grows plants in large industrial greenhouses. The growing conditions in each greenhouse are monitored and controlled by an automated computer system. The temperature in each greenhouse must be kept between 12°C and 18°C. If the temperature becomes too high cooling fans are switched on. If the temperature becomes too low heaters are switched on.

(a) Use phrases from the list on the following page to complete the flowchart showing how this system works. Some of the flowchart symbols have been labelled for you.   (4)

A   Start

B   Turn on the fans

C   Turn off the fans

D   Check the temperature inside the greenhouse

E   Is the temperature less than 12°C?

F   Is the temperature greater than 18°C?

G   Turn on the heaters

H   Turn off the heaters

I   Print out the temperature

J   Turn the water sprinklers on

K   Turn the lights on

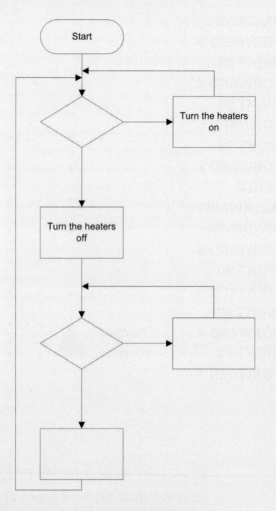

(b) Give **one** type of sensor that could be used to check the temperature inside a greenhouse. (1)

(c) How often should the system check the temperature inside a greenhouse? (1)

(d) Give **two** other **physical quantities** the system might need to monitor and control. (2)

(e) Describe **one** possible problem with the flowchart shown in part (a) and explain how it could be overcome. (2)

Web tasks

1. Visit the Free On-Line Dictionary of Computing (FOLDOC) at:
    http://wombat.doc.ic.ac.uk/foldoc/

    (a) Look up definitions of the keywords highlighted in this chapter.

    (b) Prepare a summary list of keywords and definitions to use
         for revision.

2. Visit the SMARTHOME website at:
    www.smarthome.com/sectemp.html

    (a) Read about the different types of sensor that can be used to help
         automate a home.

    (b) Choose five of the sensors and prepare a short presentation
         explaining how you would use them to help automate your
         own home.

3. Visit the Campbell Scientific website at:
    www.campbellsci.co.uk/Applications/products_in_action/prods_in_action.htm

    You will find a set of links to articles describing how
    sensors are used in computer control and monitoring systems.
    Choose **one** of these articles and prepare a summary of the key
    points. You should include a description of:

    *   the types of sensors used;
    *   the input data collected by the sensors;
    *   how the input data is processed;
    *   the output produced after processing.

Computer-aided design

Computer-aided design, or **CAD**, is the use of a computer to display designs, make changes to them and calculate and display the results. CAD has many different applications but some of the more common ones are:

- designing new cars;
- bridge and building design and testing;
- printed circuit board (PCB) design;
- designing new aircraft;
- designing fitted kitchens.

Parts of a CAD system

To run CAD software, a computer with a large memory and powerful processor is required. This is because making changes to a design requires a large number of complex calculations to be performed as quickly as possible so that their effect can be viewed straight away. Input to CAD systems is normally from a mouse and keyboard, but other input devices such as graphic tablets and scanners are also used. Output from CAD systems is produced using a high-quality printer such as a laser printer or a plotter. A CAD system also needs a high-resolution monitor so that the designer can see very clear close-up detail on the screen.

Figure CS3.1 A design produced with CAD software

In the examination you could be asked to give or choose some of the advantages of using a CAD system rather than producing designs by hand. Some possible answers are:

- *changes to a design can be made quickly and their effects seen straight away;*
- *designs can be viewed from any angle without being redrawn;*
- *designs can be tested without the need to build expensive models or prototypes;*
- *drawings of 'standard' parts can be stored on disk and used whenever they are needed. This means that new designs which will use existing parts do not have to be drawn completely from scratch;*
- *designs can be instantly sent anywhere in the world using electronic communications;*
- *designs can be used directly in computer-aided manufacturing processes.*

TIP

Computer-aided manufacture

Computer-aided manufacture, or **CAM**, is the use of a computer to control all or part of a manufacturing process. Some examples of CAM include the production of printed circuit boards, car manufacture, pattern cutting for clothing manufacture and making postage stamps. Very often a CAM process follows on directly from a CAD process: in such cases the complete design and manufacture process is called **CAD/CAM**. The main advantage of this approach is that the CAD design can be used to generate the program which will control the manufacturing process.

Figure CS3.2 A computer-controlled milling machine being used to manufacture a design prepared using a CAD package

TIP

In the examination you could be asked to give or choose some of the advantages of using a CAM system to manufacture goods. Some possible answers are:

- *products can be made very accurately and consistently;*

- *around-the-clock production is much cheaper;*

- *a product's design can be modified without the need to bring production to a complete standstill;*

- *waste can be kept to a minimum;*

- *a single human operator can oversee an entire manufacturing process;*

- *there is no need to train or employ skilled craftsmen;*

- *productivity can be greatly increased.*

Robots

Robots are used in a wide variety of manufacturing processes such as assembling or spray-painting cars. Robots all have the same basic hardware components:

- **sensors**, which are used to monitor changes in physical conditions such as speed and position;
- a **microprocessor** to process the information received from sensors;
- **actuators** to produce movement or turn external devices like switches on or off.

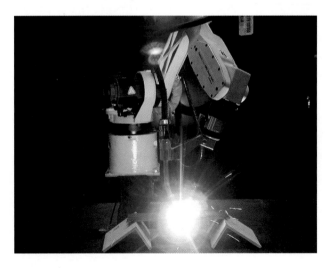

Figure CS3.3 Wanda the Welder – an industrial manufacturing robot

In the examination you could be asked to give or choose some of the advantages and disadvantages of using robots.

For the advantages, some possible answers are:

- robots can work in situations that are hazardous to humans, such as in outer space, underwater or in radioactive environments;

- robots can perform repetitive and boring tasks without needing to stop for a break;

- the quality of a robot's work is always the same, because it doesn't get tired and lose concentration;

- robots can work to a greater level of accuracy than humans;

- robots can work 24 hours a day, seven days a week, resulting in increased productivity.

The main disadvantage of robots is that they are expensive to buy and install. If a business wants to introduce new production methods, or change existing ones, it may be easier and cheaper to retrain human workers than replace them with robots.

TIP

Questions

1. Many manufacturers use CAD to help design new products.

    (a) What do the letters **CAD** stand for? (1)

    (b) Give **two** output devices needed by a CAD system. (2)

    (c) Give **one** input device, other than a keyboard or mouse, that might reasonably be used with a CAD system.

    (d) Explain why a computer with a powerful microprocessor and large memory is required in order to run CAD software. (2)

2. Many car manufacturers use CAM during their production process.

    (a) What do the letters **CAM** stand for? (1)

    (b) Give **three** advantages to the car manufacturer of using CAM. (3)

    (c) Give **two** disadvantages to the car manufacturer of using CAM. (3)

    (d) Describe **one** possible effect the introduction of CAM by a business could have on its workers. (2)

3. Robots are used in many modern manufacturing processes.

    (a) Give **three** components needed by a robot. (3)

    (b) Give **one** example of a manufacturing process that uses robots. (1)

    (c) Give **two** advantages to a manufacturer of using robots. (2)

    (d) Give **one** disadvantage to a manufacturer of using robots. (2)

    (e) Give **one** example of an application other than manufacturing where robots are used. (1)

Web tasks

1. Visit the Free On-Line Dictionary of Computing (FOLDOC) at:
    http://wombat.doc.ic.ac.uk/foldoc/

    (a) Look up definitions of the keywords highlighted in this chapter.

    (b) Prepare a summary list of keywords and definitions to use
        for revision.

2. Computer-aided design has been used to develop a wide range of virtual-reality systems.

    (a) Visit the CAD Digest website at:
        www.caddigest.com/subjects/virtual_reality/index.htm

    (b) Read about some of the virtual reality systems described there.

    (c) Prepare a short essay about one of these systems.

3. Visit the Robots home page on the Channel 4 website at:
    www.channel4.com/science/microsites/R/robots/index.html

    (a) Read the articles about robot design and construction.

    (b) Try out the robot constructor.

4. Research and prepare a presentation about **one** way that robots are being
    used other than in manufacturing. You could start by visiting these websites:

    Robot farmers
    http://web.aces.uiuc.edu/news/stories/news2813.html

    Robots in a hospital
    www.cnn.com/2004/TECH/07/06/hospital.robots.ap/index.html

The **systems life cycle** is a series of stages that are worked through during the development of a new information system. A lot of time and money can be wasted if a system is developed that doesn't work properly or do exactly what is required of it. A new system is much more likely to be successful if it is carefully planned and developed to meet needs that have been thoroughly investigated and identified. This is what the stages of the systems life cycle aim to do.

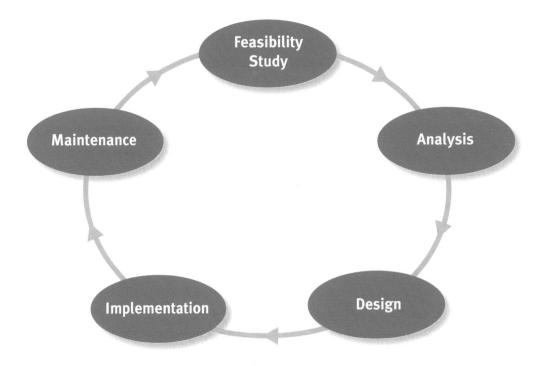

Figure 18.1 The stages of the systems life cycle

Examination questions about the systems life cycle often ask you to place the stages in the correct order. You could also be asked to give some of the activities that take place at certain stages – these are all described in this chapter.

It is normal for people to work in a group on the development of a new information system. This group is called the **system development project team**. Most of the members of this team will be **systems analysts**. A systems analyst is responsible for finding out about the existing system, designing a new system to replace it and supervising its development. The other members of the team are **programmers**. A programmer writes computer programs that match the design specifications given to them by a systems analyst.

Feasibility study

The first stage of the systems life cycle is the **feasibility study**. This is an investigation that is carried out by a systems analyst to find out what the main problems are with the existing system and if it is technically possible and cost-effective to solve these problems by developing a computer-based solution. The results of this investigation are presented by the systems analyst in a **feasibility report**, which will normally have the following contents:

- a description of the existing system, outlining what is being done and how;
- a set of **problem statements** describing exactly what the problems are with the existing system;
- a set of **system objectives**, which describe what the new system must be able to do;
- a description of some alternative solutions;
- a description of the technical, economic, legal and social factors that have been considered;
- a recommended course of action.

If the feasibility study recommends that the project should go ahead, the next stage of the systems life cycle – the analysis – can begin.

Analysis

During the analysis stage, systems analysts investigate the existing system to answer questions such as "what is being done now?", "why is it being done?", "who is doing it?" and "how is it being done?". This information is used to identify exactly what the problems are with the existing system. During an investigation, systems analysts use a variety of **fact-finding methods** to gather information. Some of the most commonly used methods are:

Questionnaires

Questionnaires are a useful way of gathering a lot of information quickly. People are often more honest and say what they really think about a system if they are filling in an anonymous questionnaire rather than being asked face-to-face in an interview. It is also much easier to analyse the responses given on a well-designed questionnaire than notes taken during interviews.

MovieZone Customer Questionnaire

This questionnaire will help us find out what you think about the service currently offered by MovieZone and try to improve it. Your opinions are very important to us. As a thank you for completing this form we will give you one night's free rental of any new release.

1. How many times a week do you rent a movie?

   ☐ Once
   ☐ Twice
   ☐ Three times
   ☐ More — please state _____

2. How easy is it to find out if we have a particular movie available for rental?

   ☐ Generally quite easy
   ☐ Generally quite difficult
   ☐ Don't know

3. Approximately how many minutes does it usually take you from choosing a movie to leaving the shop with it?

   ☐ Under 10 minutes ☐ Between 10 and 20 minutes ☐ Over 20 minutes

Figure 18.2 Part of a customer questionnaire designed to collect information from members of a video rental shop about the service they provide

Interviews

Information can be gathered by talking to people who use the existing system and asking them what they think about it. Much more detailed information can be gathered through interviews, but they can be time-consuming if a lot of people need interviewing.

Observation

Watching people use a system can often give a more accurate picture of what actually happens than using interviews or questionnaires. The problems with this method are that people can find it threatening to be watched while they are working, and quite a lot of time is needed because little useful information is gathered during short observations.

Examining documents

This method involves looking at the paperwork that is used in the existing system. Paperwork includes any forms that are completed, letters, memos and manual filing systems such as paper records in a filing cabinet. For systems that are already computerised, screen layouts and printed output will also be examined.

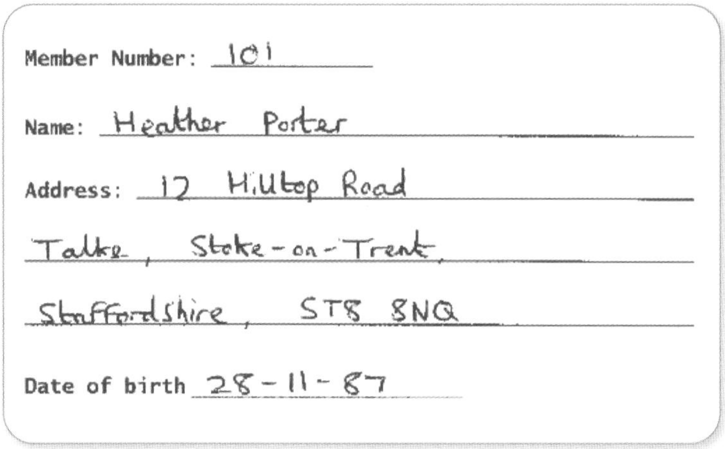

Member Number: 101

Name: Heather Porter

Address: 12 Hilltop Road

Talke, Stoke-on-Trent,

Staffordshire, ST8 8NQ

Date of birth 28-11-87

Figure 18.3 A membership card for a video rental shop – this document tells the systems analyst what information is stored about members in the current manual system

Once the systems analysts have completed their investigation, they produce a detailed description of how the existing system works. This will contain information about the data that is stored, where it is stored, how it flows around the system and how it is processed. Various methods are used by systems analysts to describe the parts of a system. These include **data flow diagrams** (or **DFDs**) and **systems flowcharts**.

A data flow diagram describes how data flows through a system. Data flow diagrams are concerned with only the data in a system and do not describe any of its hardware.

External entity – data source or data destination; for example, people who generate data such as a customer order, or receive information such as an invoice.

Process – an operation performed on the data. The two lines are optional; the top section of the box can be used to label the process, the middle to give a brief explanation, and the bottom to say where the process takes place.

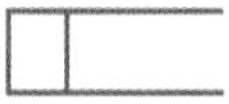

Data store – such as a file held on disk or a batch of documents.

Data flow – the arrow represents movement between entities, processes or data stores. The arrow should be labelled to describe what data is involved.

Figure 18.4 The symbols used in data flow diagrams

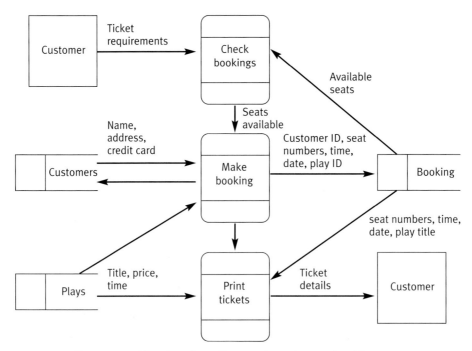

Figure 18.5 The data flow diagram for a theatre booking system

The theatre uses a computerised system to store records about customers, plays and bookings. Customers can make a booking by telephoning, visiting the booking office or completing a pre-printed form and posting it to the theatre. The booking clerk checks if there are any seats available for the performance. If there are, the clerk reserves the seats, then checks whether the customer's details are already on file and, if not, types them in. The tickets are then printed out and handed or sent to the customer. Payment is made either in cash or by credit card.

Systems flowcharts describe the parts of a system in terms of the hardware, the data that is stored, the processes that are carried out using this data and the resulting output.

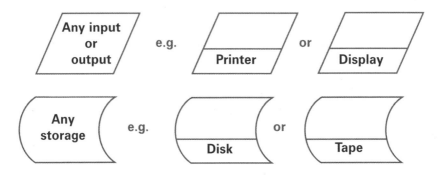

Figure 18.6 The symbols used in systems flowcharts

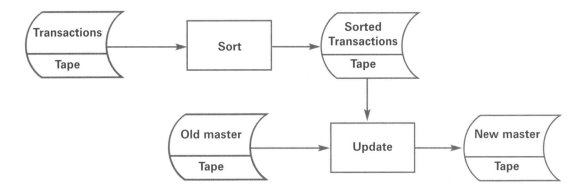

Figure 18.7 This systems flowchart represents a system where a customer file is held on tape. Receipts are held on a transaction file (also on tape) and are sorted and then used to update the master file, creating a new master file

Design

During the design stage of the systems life cycle, possible alternative solutions are identified. For example, some or all of these alternative methods might be considered:

* **Create the new system by using programming languages to write special software.**

  The advantage of this method is that programs can be designed which exactly meet the required specification. The disadvantage of this method is that it can be time-consuming and expensive.

* **Buy application software and customise it to provide a new system.**

  The advantage of this method is that commercially available software has already been thoroughly tested and can be installed quickly. This method of solution is therefore much less time-consuming than developing new software from scratch.

* **Use an application development tool to create a new system.**

  An **application development tool** provides building blocks that allow new applications to be developed much more quickly than traditional programming methods would allow.

Once alternative solutions have been identified they are evaluated by asking questions like:

* what hardware does this solution require?
* what benefits does this solution offer?

- what are the drawbacks of this solution?
- how long will it take to develop this solution?
- how much will this solution cost?

This process allows systems analysts to identify the best solution. The rest of the design stage is then concerned with producing a **design specification** that describes the new system in detail and contains information about:

Input

- what data will need to be input?
- what are the sources of the input data?
- what input methods will be used?
- what will any input screens need to look like and have on them?

Output

- what output is required from the system?
- what output methods will be used?
- what layout is needed on printed output?
- what will output screens need to look like and have on them?

Data storage

- what data files are needed?
- what fields will the records in each file need?
- what validation checks will be used to make sure data is sensible and correct?

User interface

- which type of user interface will be used (menu-driven, graphical or command-driven)?
- what options will be available to users?

Backup and recovery procedures

- what methods will be used to back up the system?
- how often will backups be carried out?
- where will backup copies be kept?
- how will data be restored if it is lost or damaged?

Security procedures

- how will data be protected from unauthorised access?
- will some users need different levels of access from other users?

Test plan

A **test plan** describing the testing to be carried out on the new system is prepared. This should include details of the purpose of each test, the test data to be used and what the expected results are. A test plan should also include space where the actual results of the testing can be recorded.

Implementation

This stage of the systems life cycle involves setting up the system described in the design specification. As we have already discussed, this may involve writing new programs, customising existing commercial software or using application development tools. Whatever the method used, some of the activities at this stage will include:

* creating data files;
* setting up data validation checks;
* entering enough data ready for testing the system;
* creating input and output screens;
* setting up the user interface;
* setting up system security.

Testing

Testing should be carried out using a test plan prepared during the design stage to make sure all the parts of a system work correctly with **normal**, **extreme** and **erroneous** data. Figure 18.8 shows a test plan that uses these types of test data. The tests shown are being used to check part of a system that must input student examination marks in the range 0 to 100.

Test No	Purpose of test	Test data	Expected result
1	Check the input mark function accepts normal data	45	Mark accepted
2	Check the input mark function accepts extreme data	0	Mark accepted
3	Check the input mark function accepts extreme data	100	Mark accepted
4	Check the input mark function rejects erroneous data	-45	Mark rejected – error message displayed

Figure 18.8 A typical test plan format

Test 1 uses **normal** test data to check that the system will accept marks within the allowed range.

Tests 2 and 3 use **extreme** test data to check that the system will accept marks on the boundaries of the allowed range – in this case 0 and 100.

Test 4 uses **erroneous** test data to check that the system will reject marks outside the allowed range.

TIP

In the examination you could be asked to distinguish between the three main types of test data. Make sure you can explain that:

- *normal test data is used to check that a system can handle the sort of data that would be expected during day-to-day use;*

- *extreme test data is used to check that a system can cope with data that lies on the boundaries of what is acceptable;*

- *erroneous (or exceptional) test data is used to check that a system can identify data that is wrong and reject it.*

Installation

This stage might include any of the following activities:

- installing new hardware and software;
- transferring data from the existing system to the new one;
- training users how to operate the new system;
- producing documentation for the new system;
- carrying out a **post-implementation review** after the new system has been running for a few weeks or months, to identify any modifications that may need to be made.

Installation methods

There are many different ways that a new information system can be introduced. Some of the most common ones are:

- **Direct changeover** involves changing from using the old system one day to using the new one the next. This is the quickest way of introducing a new system but can be very disruptive if any problems are found afterwards.

- **Pilot running** involves trying the new system out with a small group of users to identify and correct any problems before everyone starts using it.

- **Parallel running** involves operating the new system and the old system alongside each other for a short period of time. This has the advantage that problems with the new system can be sorted out without any disruption. The disadvantage of this method is that it can be difficult and stressful for staff to try and operate two systems at the same time.
- **Phased changeover** involves introducing the new system one part at a time while leaving the remaining parts of the old system in place until they are all eventually replaced.

Maintenance

After a new information system has been successfully installed and running for some time it may need to be changed. This could be due to a change in the needs of the user, to correct problems not found during testing, or simply to improve the way the system works.

Systems documentation

There are two types of systems documentation – **technical documentation** and **user documentation**.

Technical documentation describes a system in detail, in terms that a systems analyst or programmer can understand if changes need to be made to it. This will include things like:

- the systems design specification;
- systems flowcharts;
- data flow diagrams;
- a description of the various parts of the system and what each one does;
- screen layouts and user-interface designs;
- the test plan.

User documentation provides the people who will be using a system with information about what it can do, how to operate it and how to deal with error messages. Good user documentation should contain the following sections:

- a description of what the system is designed to do;
- minimum hardware and software requirements of the system;
- instructions on how to load and run the system;
- detailed instructions on how to operate each part of the system;
- error messages, their meaning and how to deal with them;
- where to get more help, such as telephone support lines and online tutorials.

Adding new member details

- Click on the **members** button   **Members**   on the **main menu**

- The **members form** will be displayed (Figure 3.1)

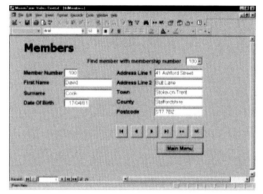

Figure 3.1

- Click on the **new record** button

- A blank form will be displayed.

- Enter the new member details by clicking in each box in turn starting with the member number and typing in the required information.

Figure 18.9 Part of the user manual for a new video rental shop system.

Review

Once a new information system has been successfully installed and running for some time it may need to be changed. This could be due to a change in the needs of the user, to correct problems not found during testing, or simply to improve the way the system works.

Questions

1. The stages of the system life cycle are shown in the diagram below.

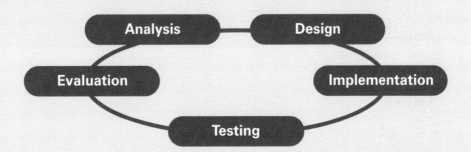

   Give the stage of system life cycle during which **each** of the activities listed would take place.

   (a) Identify the problems that need solving

   (b) Prepare a test plan

   (c) Plan the layout of data entry screens

   (d) Enter test data

   (e) Discuss how well the new system works

   (f) Set up data files

   (g) Decide which software to use

   (h) Interview users of the existing system

   (i) Suggest future improvements to the new system   (9)

   AQA (NEAB) 2002 Paper 2 Tier H

2. The system life cycle describes the stages that are worked through when a new computer system is being developed.

   (a) List the stages of the system life cycle given below in the correct order. The first one has been done for you.

   Design
   Implementation
   Analysis
   Feasibility study
   Evaluation
   Testing

Stage 1	**Feasibility study**
Stage 2	
Stage 3	
Stage 4	
Stage 5	
Stage 6	(5)

(b) Give **two** activities that would take place during the analysis stage of the system life cycle. (2)

(c) Give **two** activities that would take place during the design stage of the system life cycle. (2)

(d) Give **three** different types of test data that should be used during the testing stage of the system life cycle. (3)

(e) Give **three** topics that should be included in the user documentation for a new computer system. (3)

(f) Give **two** items that should be included in the technical documentation for a new computer system. (2)

AQA (NEAB) 2001 Paper 2 Tier F

3. The partners of a doctors' surgery are considering using a computer system to store patient records and handle appointments. A systems analyst is called in to carry out a feasibility study.

(a) Explain why a feasibility study is carried out. (3)

(b) After the feasibility study, the decision is made to go ahead with the introduction of the computer system. The systems analyst then carries out a detailed analysis of the existing system. Give **three** ways that the systems analyst could find out about the existing system. (3)

(c) After the analysis the systems analyst then produces a design specification for the new system. Give **four** items that should be included in the design specification. (4)

AQA (NEAB) 2000 Paper 2 Tier F

4. Developing a new computer system involves going through a number of different stages. These stages are called the 'system life cycle'. The stages of the system life cycle are shown in the diagram below.

Describe what happens during **each one** of these stages.

AQA (NEAB) 2000 Paper 2 Tier H

Web tasks

1. Visit the Free On-Line Dictionary of Computing (FOLDOC) at:
   http://wombat.doc.ic.ac.uk/foldoc/

   (a) Look up definitions of the keywords highlighted in this chapter.

   (b) Prepare a summary list of keywords and definitions to use
       for revision.

2. Work through and read the systems analysis fables at:
   www.umsl.edu/~sauter/analysis/analysis_links.html#fables

   The moral of each fable makes a key point about activities during the systems
   life cycle – use these to prepare a 'top ten' list of tips for producing a
   successful new information system.

A **network** is a collection of two or more computers that are connected to each other allowing them to share hardware, software and data. There are two different types of computer network – **Wide Area Networks** (or **WANs**) and **Local Area Network** (or **LANs**). A computer that is not connected to a network is called a **stand-alone** computer. Most of the computers used in homes are stand-alone computers.

LANs

Computers in a LAN are all in the same building, or in different buildings on one site. Most school networks are LANs. **Data cables** are used to connect computers, and peripheral devices like printers, to a LAN. Connections that use high-frequency radio signals, infrared light beams, or lasers are also becoming quite common. These 'wireless' connections allow portable computers to connect to a LAN; they are also useful in old buildings where it may be difficult or impossible to install cables.

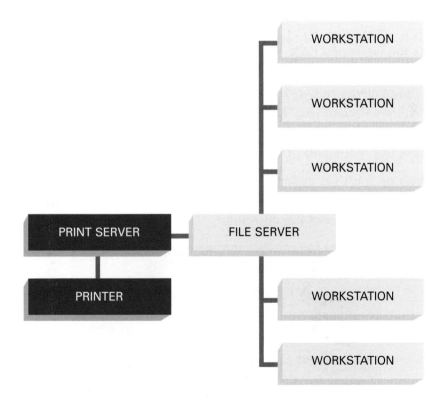

Figure 19.1 A local area network

Chapter 19

On a typical LAN application, software and users' data files are stored on a powerful central computer called a **file server** (or just **server** for short). To use a LAN you must identify yourself to the server by giving your **user identity** (or **user name**) and **password**. This is called **logging on**; when you have done this you can run programs and load any files you have saved during a previous session. Once you have finished using the network you **log off** – this disconnects you from the file server until you log on again.

Figure 19.2 A network log on screen – a username and password are needed to gain access to this network

The server is the heart of a LAN. It stores all the application software and data needed by users, manages the resources available to network users, and maintains a list of all the network users and their passwords. Servers use special operating system software (e.g. MS Windows 2000 Server) to carry out these tasks. Larger local area networks often have more than one server dedicated to particular tasks like managing printing or e-mail.

Each computer on a LAN is called a **workstation**. To connect to a LAN, a workstation must have a **network card**. This is the device through which data signals are sent in and out of the computer.

Figure 19.3 Workstations in a local area network

WANs

Computers in a WAN are spread over a large geographical area. This might be around a town, a country or even in different continents. The computers in a WAN are not permanently connected to each other with data cables; they communicate with each other using telephone lines, radio transmitters or satellite links. The Internet is an example of a WAN.

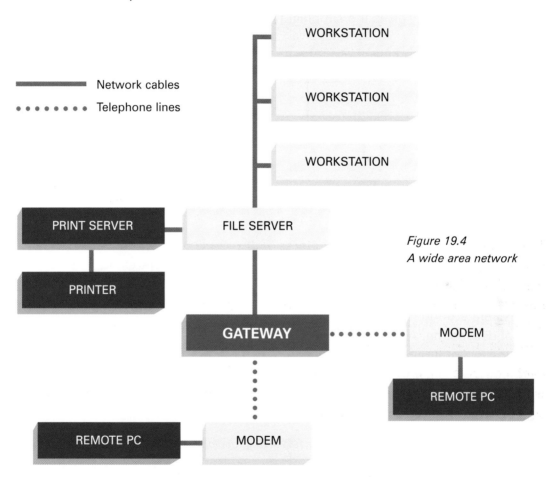

Figure 19.4
A wide area network

Unlike the computers in a LAN, the computers of a WAN are not permanently connected to each other with cables. The computers in a wide area network are often connected to each other using telephone lines. If an entire LAN needs to be connected to a WAN, a special **gateway** must be set-up. This allows any computer on the LAN to communicate with any computer on the WAN.

Make sure that you know and understand the differences between LANs and WANs - you could be asked to explain this in the examination.

TIP

Network topologies

The **topology** of a network describes the way cables are used to connect network devices like servers, workstations or printers.

Bus

In a **bus topology**, all the computers are connected through their own cable to a single central cable. This is the simplest type of topology.

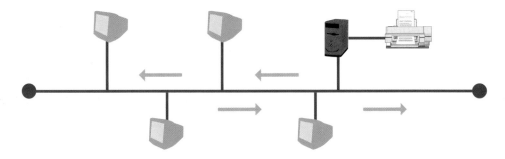

Figure 19.5 A bus topology

Ring

In a **ring topology**, computers are connected to each other in a large circle. Data is sent around the ring until it reaches its final destination. A problem with this topology is that if one computer fails the entire network will break down. This is one reason why ring topologies are not used much any more.

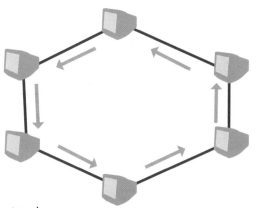

Figure 19.6 A ring topology

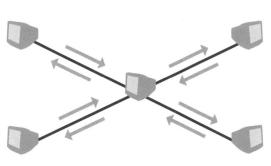

Star

In a **star topology**, each computer is connected directly to a central server by a dedicated cable. This type of topology is very reliable but the cabling can be quite expensive.

Figure 19.7 A star topology

Network security

Connecting computers together in networks increases the risk of data being tampered with, damaged, lost or stolen. The main threat to data stored on networks comes from other users and hackers gaining unauthorised access to programs and data and causing damage either deliberately or accidentally. There are a number of different security measures used on networks to protect programs and data.

Passwords

We have already mentioned that access to individual users' data on a network is protected with **user identities** and **passwords**. This is not a completely foolproof way to protect data because it is relatively straightforward to guess or 'crack' passwords. There are some simple rules that network users should follow in order to keep their passwords secure.

Do

- choose a password that is at least five characters long – if your password is too short it will be much easier for someone to watch you typing it in and remember what it is;
- use a combination of letters and numbers in your password;
- change your password regularly.

Don't

- use words that can be found in a dictionary – these can be easily found using a password-cracking program or guessed if someone sees you typing part of the word;
- use your name or nickname, date of birth, a friend's name or the name of a relative – all of these stand a good chance of being correctly guessed by anyone who knows you;
- write your password down where it can be easily found, such as underneath the keyboard.

Levels of access

Unauthorised access to data on a network can be reduced by allowing different users different **levels of access**, or **access permissions**. For example, on a school network, individual students can access only their own work but the **Network Administrator** can access any student's work.

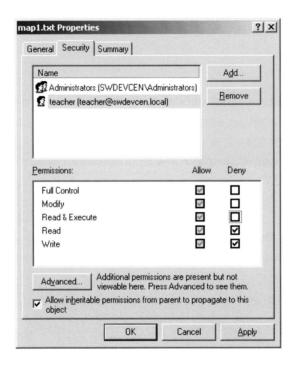

Figure 19.8 Setting access permissions for a user on an MS Windows 2000 Server

Restricting access

Local area networks can be protected by physically **restricting access** to the computer room. This is most easily done by simply locking the door or providing users with an entry code or special 'swipe card' key.

Using computers in a LAN has both advantages and disadvantages. You could be asked to give or choose some of these in the examination.

For the advantages some possible answers are:

- *Workstations can share peripheral devices such as printers. This is cheaper than buying a printer for every workstation;*

- *Workstations don't necessarily need their own hard disk or CD-ROM drives, which makes them cheaper to buy than stand-alone PC's;*

- *Users can save their work centrally on the network's file server. This means that they can retrieve their work from any workstation on the network. They don't need to go back to the same workstation all the time;*

- *Users can communicate with each other and transfer data between workstations very easily;*

- *One copy of each application package such as a word processor, spreadsheet, etc., can be loaded onto the file server and shared by all users. When a new version comes out, it only has to be loaded onto the server instead of onto every workstation.*

TIP

For the disadvantages some possible answers are:

- *Special security measures are needed to stop users from using programs and data that they shouldn't have access to;*

- *Networks are difficult to set up and must be maintained by skilled ICT technicians;*

- *If the file server develops a serious fault then all the users are affected, rather than just one user in the case of a stand-alone machine.*

Questions

1. LAN and WAN are both types of computer network.

   (a) (i) What do the letters **LAN** stand for? (1)

   (ii) What do the letters **WAN** stand for? (1)

   (b) Give **two** differences between a LAN and a WAN. (2)

   (c) Give **three** advantages to computer users of a LAN rather than working on stand-alone machines. (3)

   (d) Give **one** method which can be used to prevent the misuse of data being transferred between computers. (1)

   AQA (NEAB) 2001 Paper 2 Tier F

2. Explain briefly what is meant by the following terms.

   (a) workstation (1)

   (b) file server (1)

   (c) user identity (1)

   (d) password (1)

   (e) log on (1)

3. (a) Give **two** reasons why special security measures are needed on computer networks. (2)

   (b) Describe **two** security measures used to protect data on a computer network. (2)

4. Computers can be stand-alone or linked together to form networks. LANs and WANs are two different types of network.

   Describe the main features of **each** of these types of network and the advantages offered to users by network computers compared with stand-alone machines. (15)

   AQA (NEAB) 2002 Paper 2 Tier H

Web tasks

1. Visit the Free On-Line Dictionary of Computing (FOLDOC) at:
    http://wombat.doc.ic.ac.uk/foldoc/

    (a) Look up definitions of the keywords highlighted in this chapter.

    (b) Prepare a summary list of keywords and definitions to use
         for revision.

2. Read more about network topologies at:

    http://compnetworking.about.com/library/weekly/aa041601a.htm

3. Find out more about wireless networks at:

    www.vicomsoft.com/knowledge/reference/wireless1.html

4. For a more detailed technical introduction to Wide Area Networks visit:

    www.pulsewan.com/wanintro.htm

The Internet links private PCs, public networks and business networks together using telephone lines to form one vast worldwide network. It allows computer users to share and exchange information with each other wherever they are in the world. The information on the Internet comes in many different formats. These range from simple e-mail text files to music, video clips, computer software and even live television pictures.

Connecting to the Internet

The simplest way to connect to the Internet is to use a **dial-up connection**. This type of connection requires a computer with a modem and access to a telephone line. The **digital signals** generated by computers are made up from binary patterns of 0s and 1s and can't be transmitted along standard telephone lines. A modem converts a digital signal into an equivalent **analogue signal** so that it can be sent down a telephone line. At the destination, another modem is needed to convert the analogue signal back into a digital signal which the receiving computer can understand. This process is called **modulation-demodulation**, which is where the term **modem** comes from. The speed of a modem is measured in **kilobits per second (Kbps)** – this is a measure of how fast data can be transferred. Dial-up modem connections offer data transfer speeds of up to 56 Kbps.

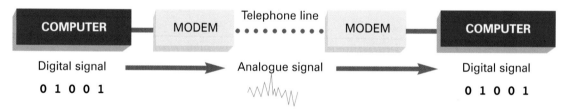

Figure 20.1 Exchanging data between computers using ordinary telephone lines and modems

A faster connection is possible with an **ISDN line (Integrated Services Digital Network)**, which is a special type of digital telephone line. ISDN lines use a device called a **terminal adaptor** instead of a modem at both ends of the connection. Some schools use ISDN lines to connect the computers on their local area networks to the Internet, but they can be expensive for home users. ISDN connections offer data transfer speeds of up to 128 Kbps.

Dial-up modems and ISDN lines are gradually being replaced by 'always-on' broadband connections that use a system called **ADSL (Asymmetric Digital Subscriber Line)**. The term 'always-on' means the Internet can be accessed at any time without having to dial a special telephone number first and wait for a connection to be established. ADSL is much faster than ISDN, typically offering data transfer speeds of between 500 Kbps and 1,000 Kbps (1 Mbps).

Some larger organisations use a **leased line** as their method of connection. A leased line is a private telephone line which is permanently open 24 hours a day. Very high speed digital lines are available but these cost hundreds of thousands of pounds per year to use.

When the computers on a local area network need to be connected to the Internet using an ISDN or leased line, a device called a **router** is needed. A router is a special piece of hardware which co-ordinates the switching of messages between the computers on the local area network and the rest of the Internet.

Over the next few years other methods of connecting to the Internet will become more common. The current generation of mobile phones allows users to view cut-down text-based versions of selected websites or send and receive e-mail; the next will allow access to any website, which will be displayed on a small touch-sensitive LCD screen. Some digital TV services now offer access to the Internet and e-mail through the television without the need for a computer.

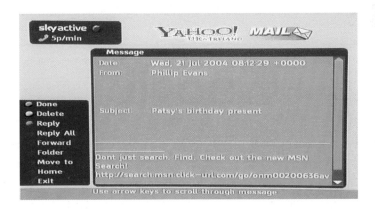

Figure 20.2 Accessing an e-mail account on digital TV

Once you have chosen a method of connection, the next step is to find an **Internet Service Provider (ISP)**. An Internet Service Provider is a commercial organisation which provides a connection to the Internet for other businesses or individuals.

ISPs charge a small monthly fee for providing a connection. Users may also need to pay for the time spent using the telephone when they are 'online'.

Surfing the Internet

The Internet can be a valuable source of information. Most libraries offer computers with Internet access, as an additional source of information to printed books.

While the Internet is a massive network for computers to communicate with each other - via e-mail for example - a large part of the Internet known as the **World Wide Web** (or just the **Web**) is a system of accessing information by means of **web pages** on websites. The user clicks on **hyperlinks** to jump from page to page and to download files

Web addresses give the location of individual sites on the **World Wide Web**. A website can be quickly accessed using its address, which is often referred to as a **URL** (or **Uniform Resource Locator**). Most URLs start with **http://www.** followed by a specific **site address** which is subdivided with full-stops and 'forward slashes' (/).

Website addresses often reveal the country of origin, such as **.uk** for the United Kingdom. They also indicate whether the site is commercial (with either **.co** or **.com**), a government organisation (with **.gov**), or an academic organisation (with **.ac**).

Search engines allow users to **surf** the Internet for information by entering **keywords**. There are a huge number of search engines available on the Internet.

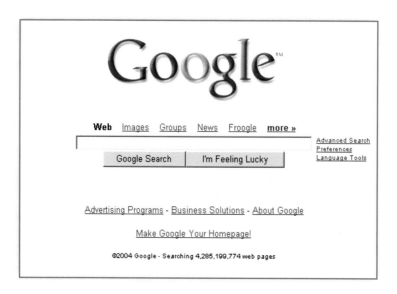

Figure 20.3 The home page of Google – the most popular search engine on the Internet

Using the Internet for research offers both advantages and disadvantages compared with more traditional methods such as using books. You could be asked about this in the examination.

Some of the advantages of using the Internet to carry out research are:

* *information is more up-to-date;*

* *information can be accessed at any time of day or night;*

* *information is available as sound and video as well as text;*

* *information can be obtained direct from experts using chat and e-mail;*

* *information is presented in electronic format allowing it to be reused (e.g. copied and pasted into a word-processed document);*

* *using the Internet is more interesting than working with books in a library.*

TIP

Some of the disadvantages of using the Internet to carry out research are:

* *some sources of information are unreliable, biased or incorrect;*

* *access to information can be slow unless an expensive high-speed connection is available;*

* *information cannot be accessed if computers break down or the Internet connection is broken;*

* *people need to know how to use a computer in order to access the information;*

* *it can take longer to find the right information compared with being told which books to look in.*

Online shopping

Many businesses now have websites that allow Internet users to buy their goods or services online at any time of day or night throughout the year. This type of shopping also offers the advantages to shoppers of not needing to travel anywhere or get pushed around in crowded shops. There are even some companies who do all of their business over the Internet and have no ordinary shops.

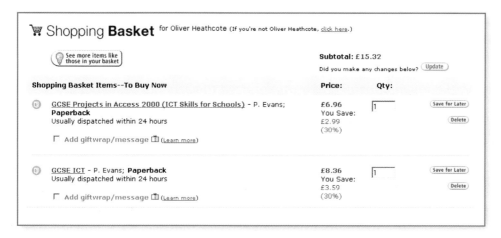

Figure 20.4 An online 'shopping basket'

Online shopping has both advantages and disadvantages. You could be asked about these in the examination.

For the advantages some possible answers are:

- money doesn't have to be spent on normal business overheads like renting shops and paying employees;

- customers can be offered a much wider choice of goods because they can be ordered from suppliers as required rather than having to be kept available on the shelves all the time;

- money is not tied up in unsold stock or wasted on products that aren't popular;

- data about customers and their buying habits can be collected directly and used to offer a much more personalised service tailored to suit the needs of each individual customer.

For the disadvantages some possible answers are:

- online transactions require users to enter a debit or credit card number before a purchase can be completed. There is a danger of these numbers being intercepted by hackers during transmission and used to make unauthorised purchases. The use of encryption and smart cards can help to protect against this;

- criminals can set up fake websites offering goods or services often using the name of a genuine company. This can lead to people spending money on goods and services that they will never receive, as well as damaging the reputation of a genuine business;

- it is much easier for a business to gather information about its rivals by simply accessing their websites – this can make it much harder to remain competitive.

TIP

Online booking

Online booking systems allow Internet users to check the availability of, and book, things like:

- theatre, cinema and concert tickets;
- seats on coaches, trains and aeroplanes;
- hotel rooms.

An online booking system is essentially a website that can be used to access a remote database. Suppose, for example, that you wanted to reserve a hotel room. If the hotel had an online booking system available on its website you would be able to specify the date of your arrival, length of stay and type of room required. This information would be sent over the Internet and used to search the hotel's room reservations database to see if any rooms were available that matched your request. If a room was available you would be able to reserve it by entering your personal details and credit card number – the details of your reservation would then be sent to the hotel and its reservations database would be updated instantly.

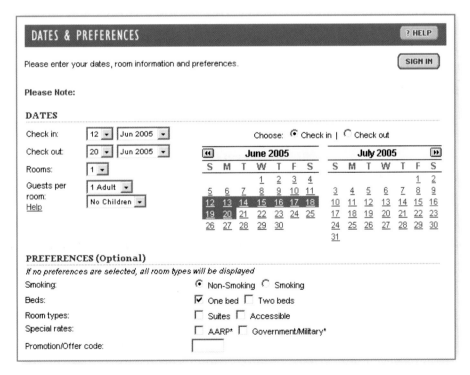

Figure 20.5 Booking a hotel room online

Online threats

Connecting to the Internet is not without its dangers: it exposes computers to threats from hackers and viruses. The threat of viruses infecting your computer is perhaps more common than that posed by hackers. Whenever you read e-mail or download files from the Internet you could also be letting viruses loose on your system. E-mail viruses, which infect your system the minute you open up a message to read it, are the most common source of virus infection on computers today.

There are also dangers in using the Internet at school and at home where children have access to it. There are a lot of websites that contain pornography and other undesirable material. Some of the measures that both schools and parents can take to prevent children from accessing undesirable websites are to:

- use software that blocks sites and prevents users from typing certain words into search engines when they are searching the web;
- supervise access to the Internet by always having an adult present when it is being used;
- use an ISP that offers a filtered service. This means that only certain 'allowed sites' can be viewed, and sites known to be a problem are blocked.

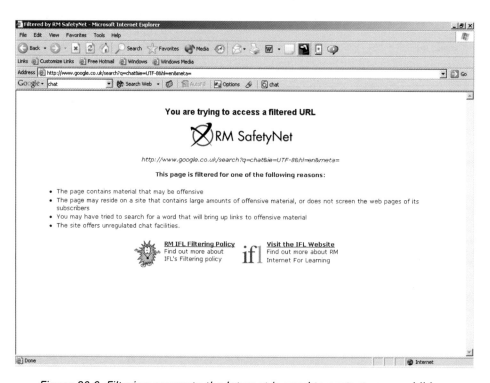

Figure 20.6 Filtering access to the Internet is used to protect young children

The Internet has both advantages and disadvantages. You could be asked to give or choose some of these in the examination.

For the advantages some possible answers are:

- *easy communication with other people all around the world;*

- *it enables more people to work from home;*

- *a vast amount of up-to-date information can be accessed;*

- *the Internet is a valuable resource for companies to advertise and conduct business.*

For the disadvantages some possible answers are:

- *much of the information isn't checked and may be incorrect or irrelevant;*

- *a large amount of undesirable material, such as pornography, is readily available;*

- *messages sent across the Internet can be easily intercepted and are open to abuse by others;*

- *too much time spent on the Internet could result in a lack of face-to-face interaction with others and a loss of social skills;*

- *going online runs the risk of hackers or viruses being able to damage your computer.*

TIP

Questions

1. John was asked to do some research on South America as part of his GCSE Geography project. He decided to use his Internet access at home and at school to find the information he needed, rather than using books from the school or local libraries.

    (a) Give **three** advantages to John in using the Internet to find the information rather than books. (3)

    (b) Give **two** advantages of using books to access the information rather than the Internet. (2)

    AQA (NEAB) 2002 (Short Course) Tier F

2. Many school libraries have computers that can be used by pupils to access the Internet.

    (a) Give **two** advantages to pupils of having computers with Internet access in the school library. (2)

    (b) Describe **one** possible way pupils could misuse the Internet. (1)

    (c) Give **two** methods a school could use to prevent pupils from misusing the Internet. (2)

3. Many businesses now offer online shopping services on their websites.

    (a) What is an *online shopping service*? (2)

    (b) Give **two** advantages to a business of selling goods online. (2)

    (c) Give **two** advantages to consumers of shopping online. (2)

    (d) Give **one** possible danger to consumers of shopping online. (1)

4. You have been asked to organise a holiday for yourself and a group of friends. Describe how the Internet could be used to help you plan and book the holiday. (5)

Web tasks

1. Visit the Free On-Line Dictionary of Computing (FOLDOC) at:
   http://wombat.doc.ic.ac.uk/foldoc/

   (a) Look up definitions of the keywords highlighted in this chapter.

   (b) Prepare a summary list of keywords and definitions to use for revision.

2. Visit **www.isoc.org/internet-history**

   (a) Use the links on this page to carry out some research about the history of the Internet.

   (b) Use the information you find to write a brief history of the Internet.

3. Search engines don't all work in the same way.

   Find out more about this by visiting:
   www.lib.berkeley.edu/TeachingLib/Guides/Internet/SearchEngines.html

   Prepare a summary of the key points.

One of the most important ways information technology is used today is to distribute, exchange and share information. Electronic communication systems are what we use to do this. The most widely used forms of electronic communication are **Viewdata, fax, e-mail, video conferencing, mobile phones, computer networks** and the **Internet**.

Viewdata

Viewdata (or **Videotext**) looks like teletext but is different because, unlike teletext, it allows two-way communication to take place. The reason for this is that videotext is transmitted along telephone lines via a **modem**. Before the Internet, Viewdata systems were used to do things like shopping from home, or book train seats, airline seats, theatre tickets and holidays. Prestel, a Viewdata system operated by BT, still allows its subscribers to do these sorts of things. Perhaps the most common use of Viewdata now is by travel agents to book holidays since many of the other things that people once used Viewdata systems like Prestel for, they can now do using the Internet.

Fax

A fax machine (originally called **facsimile**) scans paper documents and converts them into **digital format**. The digital version of whatever has been scanned is then converted into **analogue format** and sent over an ordinary telephone line to another fax machine. The fax machine at the receiving end converts the analogue information back into digital format and reproduces an exact hard copy of the original document.

Faxes are particularly useful for transferring images such as plans, drawings or documents with signatures between remote locations when it is important that an identical copy of the original is received at the other end. It is also possible to send and receive faxes using a personal computer if it has a fax-modem attached.

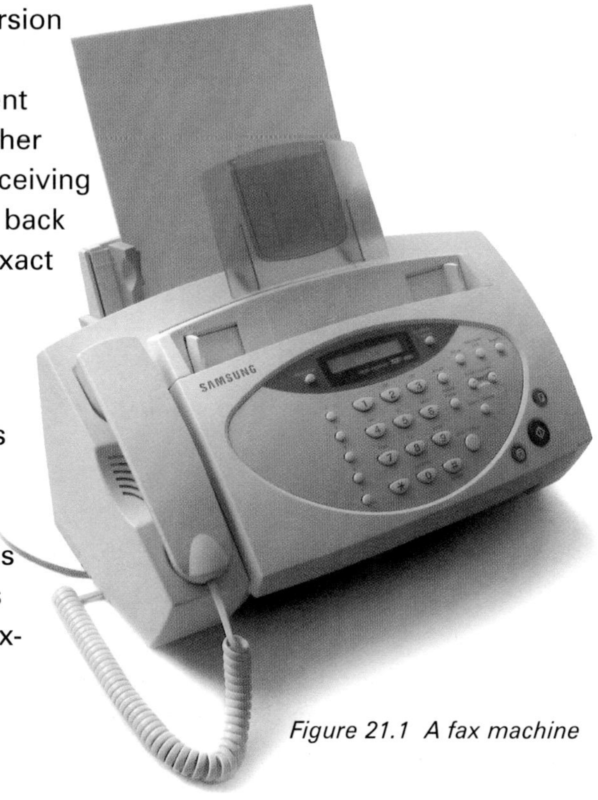

Figure 21.1 A fax machine

E-mail

E-mail (or **electronic mail**), is used to send messages from one computer to another. E-mail can be sent between computers on a local area network or between computers on the Internet.

To use e-mail, the user types in their message along with the **e-mail address** of the person that it is being sent to. The message is then converted into an electronic format by the computer. The 'electronic' version of the message is then sent (or **routed**) to its destination.

If e-mail is being sent internally on a local area network it is just transferred along the network cables. E-mail being sent between computers that are a long way from each other is transferred along communications links such as telephone lines.

Incoming messages are collected and stored by the recipient's **e-mail service provider** on a central computer called a **mail server** until they open their **electronic mailbox** and download them. Once a message has been downloaded it can be read, saved, deleted, printed out or forwarded to another user.

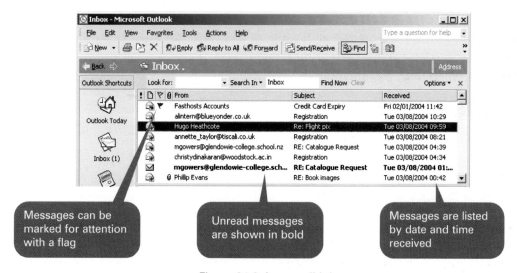

Figure 21.2 An e-mail inbox

One of the main problems with e-mail is protecting messages from being intercepted and read by hackers. Anyone who intercepts an e-mail can alter the contents and pass it on still looking as if it has come from the original sender. The privacy of e-mail messages can be protected by **encrypting** them with **digital signatures** so that only the intended recipients can read them. When the e-mail is received a message is displayed confirming that the information it contains has not been tampered with.

Sending multiple identical e-mails to thousands (or millions) of people who have not asked for them is known as **spamming**. Spam e-mails are typically used to sell fake medicines, loans and investments or to advertise pornography. Special software filters can be used to scan incoming e-mail for spam, but spammers use a variety of tricks to bypass them. Spamming can clog up mailboxes and waste a lot of time for users who must sort through and delete unwanted messages.

TIP

Using e-mail has both advantages and disadvantages. You could be asked to give or choose some of these in the examination.

For the advantages some possible answers are:

- *E-mail arrives at its destination in at most a few hours, and often in a few minutes, rather than in a day or two through the conventional post;*

- *You can send and receive e-mail anywhere in the world (and at any time) as long as you can access the Internet either with a computer, WAP-enabled mobile phone or PDA;*

- *An e-mail message can be sent to a group of people just as easily as it can be sent to just one person;*

- *Registered e-mail can be sent, which will mail the sender a confirmation when the e-mail has been opened;*

- *E-mail can be cheaper than sending mail through the post because even long documents can be sent to the other side of the world for the price of a local telephone call;*

- *You can attach a file containing, say, a scanned photograph, which can be viewed on-screen or printed out.*

For the disadvantages some possible answers are:

- *Some office workers and managers receive so many e-mails that they are unable to answer them all, and so some may simply be ignored. If they go away on holiday their mailboxes can overflow and messages may never be received;*

- *Computer viruses are often sent by e-mail and can damage your computer;*

- *People can send junk mail which you don't want, just as they can with the conventional post.*

Mobile phones

Mobile phone technology is often divided into generations: 1G, 2G, 2.5G, and 3G. The generation of a mobile phone determines the features it is able to offer. First generation (1G) mobile phones were simple analogue devices that used a communication system called **TACS (Total Access Control System)**. They have now been phased out in the UK.

Second generation (2G) mobile phones use a communications system called **GSM (Global System for Mobile Communication)**. These phones are digital devices capable of transmitting data at 9 Kilobits per second and sending text messages using the **Short Message Service (SMS)**. Many of the mobile phones currently in use are classified as 2.5 generation (2.5G). These phones use a communications system called **GPRS (General Packet Radio Services)**, which makes them capable of transmitting data at 172 Kilobits per second. This increased data transmission rate allows them to have additional functions such as browsing cut-down, text-based versions of web pages using **WAP (Wireless Application Protocol)**, and sending and receiving e-mail.

Third generation (3G) mobiles are the most advanced. They use a new communications system called **UMTS (Universal Mobile Telecommunications System)**. These phones are capable of transmitting data at speeds of up to 2 Megabits per second. This makes it possible to transfer the large amounts of data needed to allow users to make live video calls and have full high-speed Internet access.

Figure 21.3 A prototype third generation mobile phone.
Source: 3GNewsroom.com

Teleconferencing

The telephone or e-mail can be used by people to exchange information and ideas in real time. Using these forms of communication in this way is called **teleconferencing**. A more advanced form of teleconferencing is **videoconferencing**, which is the use of a computer to send sound and video images from one computer to another in real time.

To videoconference you need:

- A computer with a large memory and a fast processor, which can handle the large amount of data that video pictures contain;
- A digital video camera to capture the video pictures at your end of the link;
- A microphone or telephone hand-set to capture the sound that goes with your pictures;
- Access to an ISDN or ADSL telephone line. This is because ordinary telephone lines weren't designed to cope with the large amount of data that needs to be sent along them for videoconferencing;
- Special videoconferencing software.

Figure 21.4 Videoconferencing (Photo courtesy of www.ihets.org)

Videoconferencing has both advantages and disadvantages. You could be asked to give or choose some of these in the examination.

For the advantages some possible answers are:

- *You can communicate with other people over long distances and see them as well as hear them. Being able to see the person at the other end of the link can be very useful if you can't rely on sound (for example if you need to use sign language);*

- *Videoconferencing is more personal than just a telephone call;*

- *Businesses can use videoconferencing to hold meetings which many people can be involved in;*

- *There is less need for people to travel, which saves money and helps the environment by cutting down on pollution from cars and other non-environmentally-friendly forms of transport.*

For the disadvantages some possible answers are:

- *The hardware and software needed for a videoconferencing system are very expensive;*

- *Not many people have videoconferencing systems, so the number of people that you can communicate with is very limited;*

- *There is no substitute for a face-to-face meeting. Eye contact and body language can be as important in a business meeting as on your first date with someone!*

TIP

Teleworking

Teleworking (or **telecommuting**), is made possible by electronic communications. Telecommuting is when people work from home instead of travelling to work and use methods of electronic communication such as the telephone, fax machine, e-mail, the Internet and videoconferencing to communicate with the outside world. In spring 2001 a government survey reported that there were 2.2 million teleworkers in the UK.

TIP

Telecommuting has both advantages and disadvantages. You could be asked to give or choose some of these in the examination.

For the advantages some possible answers are:

- *Time isn't wasted travelling to and from work;*

- *Cars are kept off the roads which helps the environment;*

- *Working at home is less stressful and it is much easier to concentrate;*

- *Working hours are more flexible and can be fitted around other things that need doing, such as collecting children from school;*

- *People who live long distances away from each other can work together without having to meet in person;*

- *Businesses need smaller offices and spend less on light and heating.*

For the disadvantages some possible answers are:

- *Workers may miss the company of their co-workers and feel isolated;*

- *Having your workplace at home might mean that you end up doing too much work and not having enough time off;*

- *It is more difficult for managers to monitor and control the workforce.*

Questions

1.   (a) What is meant by the term **e-mail**?   (1)

            (b) Give **two** items of hardware needed to use e-mail.   (2)

            (c) Do you think e-mail will ever completely replace the ordinary post? Explain your answer carefully.   (2)

2.   More and more businesses are using e-mail (electronic mail) as a method of communication with their customers. Give **two** advantages with reasons for using e-mail compared with other methods of communication such as fax or telephone or post.   (4)

                                        AQA (NEAB) 2000 Paper 1 Tier H

3.   A teacher uses the Internet to communicate with students who cannot come to school by sending them e-mail.

            (a) Give **three** advantages, other than cost and speed, of using e-mail to communicate rather than the telephone.   (3)

            (b) Give **two** disadvantages of using e-mail in this way.   (2)

            (c) Give **two** other ways that a student could use the Internet to help with schoolwork at home.   (2)

                                          AQA (NEAB) 2001 Paper 2 Tier F

4.   (a) What is meant by the term **videoconferencing**?   (2)

            (b) Give **four** advantages of videoconferencing.   (4)

            (c) Give **one** disadvantage of videoconferencing.   (1)

5.   Explain what is meant by the term **teleworking** and briefly discuss some of its possible benefits and drawbacks.   (5)

Web tasks

1. Visit the Free On-Line Dictionary of Computing (FOLDOC) at:
    http://wombat.doc.ic.ac.uk/foldoc/

    (a) Look up definitions of the keywords highlighted in this chapter.

    (b) Prepare a summary list of keywords and definitions to use for revision.

2. Carry out some research to find out how spammers get hold of e-mail addresses. Use the article and links at **www.private.org.il/harvest.html** as a starting point. Prepare a short summary of your findings.

3. Visit **www.videoconference-bureau.com/** and read through the seven reasons to use videoconferencing.

4. Visit the Knowledge Network Explorer website at:
    www.kn.pacbell.com/wired/vidconf/ideas.html#courses
    Read about some of the ways video conferencing can be used by schools.

5. Prepare a one-page fact sheet about how digital signatures work, using the information at **www.youdzone.com/signature.html**

Many businesses are now so dependent on the data that is stored on their computer systems that if it were lost or damaged they would find it very hard to carry on as normal. When data is lost or damaged it is usually due to human error. Sometimes data is damaged deliberately or even stolen. It is important that businesses take steps to protect data from being stolen, lost or damaged. They must also make sure that they can get their data back if anything ever does happen to it. The spread of information and communication technology (or ICT) has resulted in an increase in the misuse of data that is stored electronically.

In the examination you could be asked why it is often easier to misuse data stored on a computer rather than in conventional paper-based records. Some possible answers are:

- *alterations can be made without leaving a trace;*

- *very large amounts of data can be stored and searched quickly;*

- *data can be instantly transferred to other locations using e-mail and the Internet;*

- *communication links used to connect computer systems together are vulnerable to attack from **hackers**;*

- *programs like **viruses** and **logic bombs** can be designed to deliberately cause damage to computer systems.*

TIP

Hackers

A **hacker** is someone who uses their knowledge of computers to break into other computer systems. Many hackers do this simply because they enjoy the challenge. Hackers can gain remote access to any computer that is on the other end of an open connection to the Internet. Special **firewall software** can be installed on computers to try and prevent unauthorised access by providing a barrier between them and rest of the Internet.

Once a hacker has broken into a computer system they often just leave harmless messages to show that they've been there. Some hackers, however, are not so easily satisfied and will deliberately try to cause damage to the computer system that they have broken into. They will often try to do this by deleting important files. In 1990 the UK government introduced a law called The Computer Misuse Act, which made hacking illegal.

In the examination you could be asked to explain what hacking is and how the law tries to control it. Your answer should include these points:

- *hacking is unauthorised access to a computer system;*

- *the 1990 Computer Misuse Act made hacking illegal;*

- *hackers face a fine of up to £2000 and six months in prison if prosecuted.*

Viruses

A virus is a program that can make copies of itself in order to 'infect' other computers. A virus attaches itself to a program or file and then copies itself into other programs and files with which it comes in contact. When a virus runs it may do no real damage or it can do something really nasty such as re-format a hard drive. What a virus does depends on the amount of damage the virus writer wants it to cause. Viruses can spread from one computer to another by way of infected disks, files downloaded from the Internet and e-mail. E-mail viruses have had a particularly devastating effect on businesses in recent years. Examples include the Melissa and ILOVEYOU viruses, which both forced many large companies like Microsoft to completely turn off their e-mail systems until they had been contained. In the UK anyone causing damage to computer software or data with a virus can be prosecuted under the Computer Misuse Act and face five years in prison and an unlimited fine.

Origination
A programmer writes a program - the virus - to cause mischief or destruction. The virus is capable of reproducing itself.

Transmission
Often, the virus is attached to a normal program. It then copies itself to other software on the hard disk.

Reproduction
When another floppy disk is inserted into the computer's disk drive, the virus copies itself on to the floppy disk

Infection
Depending on what the original programmer wrote in the virus program, a virus may display messages, use up all the computer's memory, destroy data files or cause serious system errors.

Figure 22.1 How computer viruses are spread

There are many different types of computer virus but one of the most common types is the **macro virus**. A macro virus uses the built-in **macro language** available in most common word processing, spreadsheet and database applications. It gets onto a computer system by attaching itself to a **template file, document** or **e-mail** and running when the file is opened or closed. Macro viruses are a big problem on the Internet with over 1000 different types in existence. The reason macro viruses are such a problem is that they can be written very easily, and infected documents are rapidly transferred to other computer systems. Common examples of macro viruses are W97M.Melissa, W97M.NiceDay and W97M.Groov.

Virus-scanning software can be used to protect computer systems from infection by viruses. It does this by looking for the unique **footprints** of known viruses. Every virus infects a computer system in its own special way and leaves tell-tale signs of its presence. When a virus scanner detects a virus footprint, it deactivates the virus and removes it from the computer system.

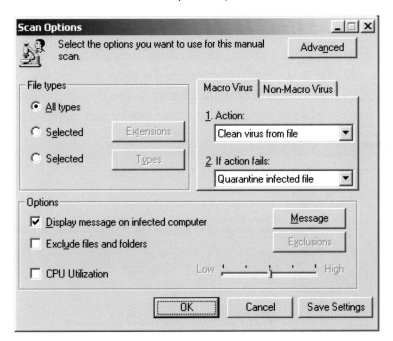

Figure 22.2 Setting up a virus scan on a personal computer

Most virus-scanning software can be set up to scan files when they are opened, downloaded from the Internet or copied. The main problem with any virus scanner is keeping its list of known viruses up-to-date, as lots of new viruses appear every day. There are currently over 50,000 known viruses in circulation. For virus-scanning programs to be effective their list of known viruses needs to be updated at least once a month. Many virus scanning packages now include a facility to download live updates to their database of virus definitions whenever a computer is online.

Logic bombs

A **logic bomb** is a set of instructions written in computer code that can be hidden inside other software and set to activate at a particular date and time. Once activated, a logic bomb will take control of a computer and begin damaging or even deleting data files. Criminals use this type of threat to blackmail businesses into giving them money by claiming they have planted a logic bomb and demanding money to call off the attack.

Software piracy

The theft of software, or **software piracy**, is a big problem for companies who produce computer software. Software piracy is when illegal copies of software are made to sell or to use, without paying the company who originally produced the software. The process of developing and testing new software before it is released is very expensive and software piracy costs companies a lot of money from lost sales. Software manufacturers often supply special unlocking codes, or **'keys'**, with their products to try and combat software piracy. In the UK, **copyright law** makes it illegal to make extra copies of software, to either use or sell, without permission.

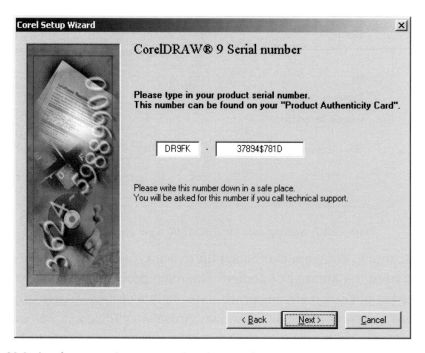

Figure 22.3 A software package prompting the user for an unlocking key during installation

In the examination you could be asked to explain why software cannot be copied without permission. Your answer should include these points:

- *UK copyright law makes it illegal to make or use unauthorised copies of software or manuals;*

- *breaking copyright law can result in up to two years in prison and unlimited fines.*

Backing up data

Backup copies are kept so that if data is lost, stolen or damaged it can be restored to its original condition. Backup copies should always be kept in a secure, airtight and heatproof container at a location remote from the computers holding the data. This is so that if data is lost due to some natural disaster like a fire or flood the backup copies will still be safe. It is also important to make backup copies of data regularly. If backup copies aren't made often enough it will be impossible to restore the data to its original condition. When backups are being made on a network it is normal to back up just the users' data files at the end of every day and all the programs and users' data files at least once a week. This is because the users' data changes more often than the programs on the network and backing up everything can take a lot of time.

Log files

A log file can be used to help track down people who have stolen or caused damage to data on a computer system. A log file records every attempt to log on to a computer, whether or not it was successful. The user identity and attempted time of log-on will be stored in the log file. If a log-on is successful, a log file will keep a record of all the files that a user has accessed and the time of any changes that are made. If someone is trying to hack into a system by dialling-in using a modem, some log files will keep a record of the telephone number.

Passwords

Passwords are often used to restrict access to data on computer systems. Some software packages allow users to **password protect** individual data files. This stops anyone who doesn't know the correct password from opening a file.

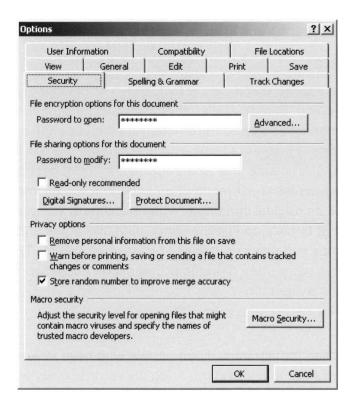

Figure 22.4 Password-protecting a document in MS Word

Some password systems are **hierarchical**. This means that different passwords will give different **levels of access** to data. At the lowest level of access a password will allow just **read-only** access to some data. Read-only access means that data can be used but not changed. The next level of access might be one that allows **read-write** access to some data. Read-write access means that data can be used and changed. The highest possible level of access is a password that allows access to read, change or even delete data anywhere on a computer system. Normally only a small number of people – like system administrators – will have this level of access.

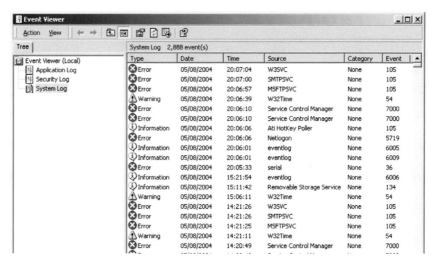

Figure 22.5 Part of a network log file

Physical security

Physical security is all about protecting data by restricting access to the computers that the data is being stored on. This is usually done by locking computer rooms and controlling access to them. Access to rooms can be controlled by putting special keypad locks on doors so that a code number must be entered before the lock will be released. Some systems use key cards with magnetic stripes on them, which have to be swiped through a magnetic stripe reader at the side of the door before the lock will be released.

Encryption

Encryption is a way of preventing data files that contain sensitive information from being used if they are stolen. **Encrypted data** is coded in such a way that it cannot be read unless special decoding (or **decryption**) software is used. Encryption is often used on the Internet to protect data when it is sent from one computer to another. If someone is buying something on a secure website, their credit card details are encrypted before being transmitted. This is to stop other Internet users from intercepting the data and using it.

Figure 22.6 Encrypting data

In the examination you could be asked to explain how data can be lost or damaged. Some possible answers are:

- due to natural hazards such as fires, floods or lightning;

- as a result of human error;

- as a result of hacking;

- due to damage caused by viruses;

- due to hardware failure (e.g., a hard disk crashing)

- due to the physical theft of disks or other computer hardware.

TIP You could also be asked to suggest precautions that could be taken to protect data and minimise the impact that any loss of data might have.

Some possible answers are:

- make regular backups of data;

- provide regular training for staff using ICT systems;

- restrict access to data, using passwords;

- encrypt data when it is being transferred across the Internet;

- lock computer rooms and restrict access to them;

- use virus-checking software regularly and keep virus definitions up-to-date.

Questions

1. A dentist stores the details of all patients on the hard disk of the practice's computer. It is important that the data stored is kept secure.

   (a) Give **three** examples of ways in which the data stored on this computer system could be lost or damaged. (3)

   (b) Give **two** physical precautions that could be taken to keep the data **secure**. (2)

   (c) Describe **one** way in which software could be used to restrict access to patient information. (1)

   AQA (NEAB) 2002 (Short Course) Tier F

2. Tanya Turner wants to use e-mail to transfer some work created on her home computer to the school network.

   (a) Give **one** possible danger to the school network of allowing pupils to transfer files using e-mail. (1)

   (b) Describe **one** precaution that both the school and its pupils could take to avoid this problem. (2)

   (c) After transferring the files Tanya discovered that she could not open them because the computers on the school network did not have the correct software installed. Tanya has asked the school's network manager if she can bring in a copy of the software on a CD so that it can be installed on the school network.

      (i) Give **one** reason why it might not be a good idea for Tanya to make a copy of the software. (1)

      (ii) Give **two** reasons why the school's network manager might refuse Tanya's request. (2)

Chapter 22

3. Data stored on computers can be damaged or even lost completely. This can have a serious effect on the individuals or businesses concerned.

    (a) Explain how data stored on a computer can become lost or damaged. (8)

    (b) Describe the precautions that an individual or business should take to minimise the effect that the damage or loss of data has on them. (8)

    AQA (NEAB) 2001 Paper 2 Tier H

4. Computer viruses have caused many problems for computer users in recent years.

    (a) What is a computer virus? (2)

    (b) Give **two** examples of ways in which a computer could become infected with a virus. (2)

    (c) Give **two** precautions that could be taken to protect a computer from viruses. (2)

    AQA (NEAB) 2002 Paper 2 Tier F

Web tasks

1. Visit the Free On-Line Dictionary of Computing (FOLDOC) at:
   http://wombat.doc.ic.ac.uk/foldoc/

   (a) Look up definitions of the keywords highlighted in this chapter.

   (b) Prepare a summary list of keywords and definitions to use for revision.

2. Prepare a summary of one of the computer misuse case studies you will find at:
   http://199.111.112.137/others/seminar/notes/crime2.html
   www.computerweekly.com/Issue398.htm

3. Find out more about viruses, worms, and Trojan Horses at:
   www.microsoft.com/athome/security/viruses/virus101.mspx

4. Identity theft and spyware are becoming increasing problems.

   (a) Visit **www.spywareguide.com/articles/identity-theft.html** to find out more.

   (b) Prepare a short presentation to outline the problems caused by identity theft and spyware.

Because large amounts of data can be transferred electronically from one ICT system to another with ease, special laws are needed to protect individuals from its misuse. In the United Kingdom a law called **The Data Protection Act** describes the rights of **data subjects** and sets out the rules that organisations collecting, storing and processing **personal data** must follow.

Personal data is any data that refers to a living, identifiable individual. Data subjects are the individuals or groups of people the personal data is about. Problems can arise when personal data is incorrect or out of date. You could, for example, be refused credit, turned down for a job, denied social security benefits or even wrongfully arrested.

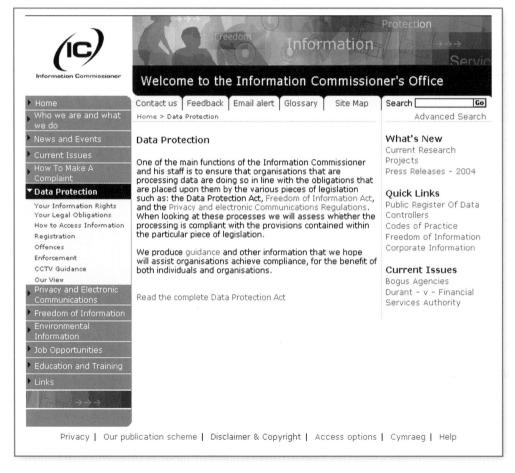

Figure 23.1 The Data Protection website provides information for data controllers and data subjects

The Data Protection Act applies to paper records as well as those stored on computers. The Data Protection Act first became law in 1984 and was updated in 1998. The new Act came into force on 1st March 2000.

Data controllers

Organisations that use personal data must have a **data controller**. This is the person in the organisation responsible for storing and processing the personal data. Data controllers must register with the **Information Commissioner** and provide information about:

- the data being collected and processed;
- the purposes for which the data will be used;
- people or organisations the data might be passed on to;
- whether the data will be transferred to any countries outside the European Union.

There are exemptions to the Data Protection Act for which registration with the Information Commissioner is <u>not</u> required – these cover data held for:

- national security purposes;
- assessing and collecting taxes;
- detecting and preventing crime;
- artistic, historical or research purposes;
- personal or domestic use (including recreational purposes);
- staff administration, accounting, advertising and marketing.

Data controllers must obey eight principles of good information handling:

1 data must be obtained and processed fairly and lawfully;

2 data must be held and processed only for stated purposes;

3 data should be adequate, relevant and not excessive for the stated purpose;

4 data must be accurate and up-to-date;

5 data must not be kept any longer than necessary;

6 data must be processed in accordance with the rights of data subjects;

7 data must be kept secure;

8 data must not be transferred to countries outside the European Union without adequate protection.

The Information Commissioner

The **Information Commissioner** – formerly the Data Protection Commissioner – is an independent officer, appointed by the Queen, who reports directly to Parliament and oversees the Freedom of Information Unit and the implementation of the Data Protection Act in the UK. The duties of the Commissioner include:

- maintaining a register of the information provided by all data controllers;
- considering complaints from data subjects about data controllers;
- prosecuting or serving notices on data controllers who have not followed the principles of information handling.

Data subjects

The Data Protection Act gives data subjects the right to:

- have a copy of all the data held about them;
- have inaccurate data corrected or deleted;
- prevent the processing of data that could result in personal distress;
- prevent the data from being used for direct marketing;
- prevent automated decisions being made based on data held about them;
- compensation for any damage or distress caused;
- ask the Information Commissioner to investigate if they feel any of the principles of information handling have not been followed.

To find out what information is held about them, a data subject must write to the person or organisation they believe holds the information and ask for a copy of all the data held about them. An example of a letter that could be used by a data subject is shown below.

Dear Sir,

Please send me the information that I am entitled to under section 7(1) of the Data Protection Act 1998. If you need further information from me, or a fee, please let me know as soon as possible.

If you do not normally handle these requests for your organisation, please pass this letter to your Data Protection Officer or another appropriate official.

Yours faithfully,

Data subjects can normally see all the data held about them but there are some exceptions if providing the information would be likely to affect:

• crime prevention or detection;

• the prosecution of offenders;

• tax collection;

• health or social work reports;

• confidential personal references.

The copy of the data can be sent as a computer printout, in a letter or on a form. It must be easy to understand and must include a description of why the data is processed and anyone it may be passed to or seen by.

Data controllers should reply within 40 days as long as the data subject has provided sufficient proof of their identity and paid any necessary fee, which must not be more than £10. If a reply is not received within 40 days, the organisation should be sent a reminder by recorded delivery. If they still don't reply or if the data received is wrong or incomplete, the Information Commissioner can help make sure the data subject gets a reply. If one of the principles of good information handling has been broken, action can be taken against the data controller to put things right.

To prepare for an examination question about the Data Protection Act make sure that you know and understand:

• *the principles of good information handling;*

• *the rights of data subjects;*

TIP

• *how data subjects can obtain a copy of data held about them;*

• *the exemptions to the Data Protection Act.*

Questions

1. Describe three rights given to data subjects by the 1998 Data Protection Act.

    (3)

    AQA 2003 (Short Course) Higher Tier

2. A music company that sells CDs by mail order has a computer system that stores personal data about its customers on a database.

    (a) Give **three** fields (other than the name and address) which the company may reasonably wish to include in the database. (3)

    (b) Personal information stored by the computer may be inaccurate. Give **two** examples of inaccuracies which could occur and, for each, describe a possible consequence for the customer. (4)

    (c) The company must be registered under the Data Protection Act 1998. Give **two** rights the Data Protection Act gives to customers. (2)

    (d) Tick **three** boxes to show which of the following are exemptions to the 1998 Data Protection Act.

	Tick **three** boxes only
Data the customer does not want anyone to see.	
Data held for domestic purposes.	
Data held by banks or building societies.	
Data where National Security is concerned.	
Data used for research, history and statistics.	
Data that does not involve numbers.	

(3)

AQA (NEAB) 2002 (Short Course) Tier F

3. A doctor's surgery stores personal data about its patients on a computer system.

    (a) Give **three** items of personal data, other than name, address and telephone number, that you would expect the surgery to store about patients. (3)

    (b) Describe the steps that the surgery should take to ensure that it complies with the Data Protection Act. (5)

    (c) Some of the patients have objected to data being stored about them on the computer and demanded to see it. Do they have an automatic right to see this data? (2)

4. For each organisation listed below give **two** items of personal data (other than name, address and telephone number) you would expect it to store about individuals.

    (a) credit reference agency

    (b) telephone company

    (c) employer

    (d) bank or building society

    (e) tax office

    (f) driver and vehicle licensing authority (DVLA) (12)

5.   (a) Who or what is the **Information Commissioner**? (2)

    (b) Describe three duties the Information Commissioner performs. (6)

6. Explain how you should go about getting a copy of the personal data held about you by an organisation on its computer system. (3)

Web tasks

1. Find out more about the UK Data Protection Act and the activities of the Information Commissioner by visiting the official website at: **www.informationcommissioner.gov.uk/**

   (a) Look up definitions of the keywords highlighted in this chapter.

   (b) Prepare a summary list of keywords and definitions to use for revision.

Health risks

Working with computers for long periods of time can cause many different kinds of health problems. These can include stress, eyestrain and injuries to the wrists, neck and back. Employers must take steps to protect employees whose work involves the regular use of computers from these health risks, or face the risk of being sued for compensation. Some of the common health risks associated with computers are described below.

Stress

Stress brought on through the use of computers is one of the major causes of work-related illness. For some people just the thought of working on a computer can give them stress. A survey, commissioned by the technology firm ICL, measured the stress levels of 200 people caused by their use of computers. It asked them how computer faults compared with other stressful situations. According to the study, 68 percent of those surveyed said visiting the in-laws was less stressful than a computer crash and one third said they would rather baby-sit! Some of the ways ICT systems can cause stress for workers are:

- Many people are afraid of computers and fear that they will be left behind or made redundant if they are unable to learn new ICT skills quickly enough and keep up with the younger more computer-literate generation.

- ICT systems make information instantly available wherever you are. Mobile phones, pagers, portable computers and the Internet make it possible to work anywhere. This means that some people find it virtually impossible to forget about work and relax.

- The amount of information that ICT systems can produce is often far too much for anyone to take in. This results in 'information overload', which causes workers to become stressed by the feeling that they can't cope with the information that they are receiving.

- Workers can be monitored using ICT systems – the feeling this causes of being constantly 'watched' can be very stressful.

Repetitive Strain Injury

Repeating the same physical movements over and over again can cause a condition known as **Repetitive Strain Injury (RSI)**. For regular computer users it is the repeated key-presses on the keyboard and long periods of holding and moving a mouse which cause a build-up of damage to the hands, arms and shoulders. Some of the more common symptoms of RSI are:

- tightness, aching or stiffness in the arms, neck or shoulders;
- numbness, coldness, or tingling in the arms and hands;
- clumsiness or loss of strength in the hands.

Sitting in the correct position, using specially designed furniture, keyboards and wrist rests, and learning how to type correctly, can all help to avoid RSI or at least reduce the damage that might be caused. Adopting a correct typing technique, for example, includes trying to do the following:

- rest your wrists on something suitable when you're typing;
- bend your wrists to the side, up or down;
- keep your wrists in the same position and stretch your fingers to hit keys, instead of moving your hands around.

Eyestrain

Spending long periods of time in front of a computer screen can cause eyestrain. This may be experienced as pain in the eyes, watering, blurred or double vision and headaches. Although there is no evidence that eyestrain causes any permanent damage, its symptoms can be very uncomfortable and distressing. Eyestrain can be avoided by making sure that there is enough light in the workplace, reducing the amount of glare from light being reflected off computer screens and making sure that the correct prescription glasses are worn by any workers who need them.

Extremely low frequency radiation

We are exposed to extremely low frequency (or **ELF**), radiation every day from sources such as the sun, the earth's magnetic field and even electricity mains at home and in the workplace. Computer monitors are also a common source of ELF. Some studies have shown that this type of radiation may cause health problems. There is some evidence, for example, that working for long periods in front of computer screen may increase the risk of a miscarriage during pregnancy.

In the examination you could be asked to give some health risks associated with the prolonged use of computers and suggest precautions that can be taken to avoid them. A possible answer could include these points:

Risk1: *Repetitive Strain Injury (RSI).*
Precaution: Fit computer keyboards with wrist rests.

Risk2: *Eyestrain.*
Precaution: Ensure the workplace is well lit.

The Health and Safety Executive

Laws that are designed to protect people from health hazards in the workplace are administered in the UK by a government body called the **Health and Safety Executive**, or **HSE**. The particular law relating to the use of computer screens is called the **Health and Safety (Display Screen Equipment regulations) 1992**.

This legislation requires *employers* to:

- inspect workstations to make sure that they meet the required standards for health and safety;
- train employees to use workstations correctly;
- make sure that employees take regular breaks or changes in activity;
- provide regular eye tests for workstation users and pay for prescription glasses.

This legislation requires *employees* to:

- use workstations and equipment correctly in accordance with the training provided by their employer;
- inform their employer of any problems relating to Health and Safety as soon as they arise, and co-operate with the correction of these problems.

The manufacturers of computer hardware must also make sure that their products comply with this legislation. For example, screens must tilt and swivel and keyboards must be separate and moveable.

Furniture and equipment

The health and safety laws relating to the use of computer equipment in the workplace also set minimum standards that furniture and equipment must meet. When purchasing new equipment or designing a working ICT environment, employers must give consideration to:

Lighting

The workplace should be well lit so that light reflected from computer screens does not cause glare, which can lead to eyestrain. Adjustable blinds should be provided at windows. Computers should be positioned so that they do not face or back onto windows.

Furniture

Height-adjustable swivel chairs with backrests should be provided and positioned at the correct height and distance from the desk and keyboard. Desks should be large enough to hold both the computer and any paperwork. Adjustable document holders must be provided so that awkward repetitive head movements can be avoided when entering data.

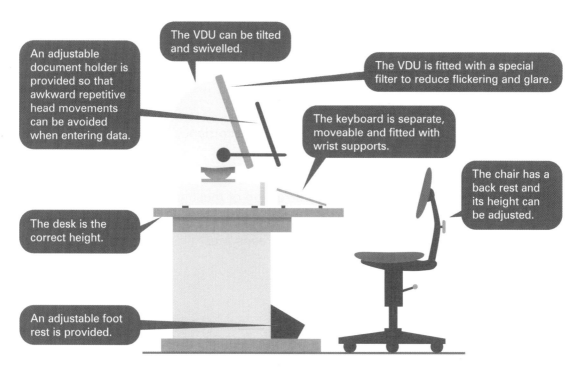

Figure 24.1 Some of the features a well-designed computer workstation should incorporate

Noise

The work space should be quiet, and noisy devices such as dot-matrix printers should be fitted with acoustic hoods or moved to a separate room.

Hardware

Screens must not flicker, and should tilt and swivel. Keyboards must be separate, moveable and fitted with wrist supports.

Software

Software should make easier the tasks that employers require employees to perform. It must be easy to use and adaptable to the user's experience.

The working environment

The work space should be well ventilated and maintained at a comfortable temperature and humidity with air conditioning and heating.

Questions

1. More people are making increased use of computers both at work and at home. This has made people more aware of computer-related health issues.

    (a) Outline **two** health problems that can occur as a result of people using a computer for long periods of time. (2)

    (b) Describe what steps can be taken to help overcome **one** of the problems you have outlined in (a) above. (2)

    AQA 2003 (Short Course) Foundation Tier

2. Laws designed to protect people from health hazards in the workplace are administered in the UK by a government body called the Health and Safety Executive.

    (a) Describe **three** obligations that the law places on employers to protect workers who operate computer terminals from possible health risks. (3)

    (b) Describe **two** obligations that the law places on employees who operate computer terminals to protect themselves from possible health risks. (2)

3. The introduction of computers into the workplace has resulted in a large increase in the number of people forced to take sick leave through stress-related illnesses. Describe how the use of computers at work can be a source of stress for many employees. (8)

4. Describe **five** factors that should be considered when designing a workplace for computer operators. Your answer should pay particular attention to the ways in which a well-designed workplace can help to avoid the health risks associated with the prolonged use of computer terminals. (10)

Web tasks

1. There are a large number of websites that offer advice for employers about using computers safely in the workplace.

    (a) Research the advice given on some of these sites – use this link to get started:
        www.businesslink.gov.uk/bdotg/action/layer?r.l2= 1074446317&r.l1=1073861197&r.s=tl&topicid=1074185088

    (b) Prepare a briefing of key points for a business considering introducing computers into the workplace.

2. Visit the BBC News website and read these articles about computer-related health issues:

    http://news.bbc.co.uk/1/hi/health/1041677.stm

    http://news.bbc.co.uk/1/hi/health/243589.stm

    http://news.bbc.co.uk/1/hi/health/142942.stm

    http://news.bbc.co.uk/1/hi/health/395348.stm

ATMs

Banks use mainframe computers to maintain their customer accounts by dealing with the transactions generated as a result of withdrawals and deposits. Each bank mainframe is also used to operate a network of **automated teller machines** (or **ATMs**), which customers can use to gain access to their accounts at any time of the day or night. Typically, an ATM can be used to:

- withdraw cash;
- check an account balance;
- order a statement or print a 'mini statement';
- order a cheque book.

Screen for diplaying available options and instructions.

Keys used for choosing options shown on the screen.

Keyboard for entering PIN and other choices.

Slot for dispensing printed receipts.

Slot where debit or credit card is inserted - this is a magnetic stripe reader.

Slot used for dispensing cash.

Figure CS4.1 The parts of an ATM

To use an ATM, a debit or credit card must be inserted in the machine, which reads an account number from the magnetic stripe on the back of the card. The ATM then asks the customer to enter their **personal identification number** (or **PIN**). This is a security measure, which is used to prevent unauthorised access to accounts. The customer is given only three attempts to enter the correct number before the ATM retains the card. If a correct PIN is entered, the customer is asked to select the option that they require from an on-screen menu, which lists the available choices. If cash is being withdrawn the amount must be entered and the ATM checks the current balance of the customer's account to see if they have enough money. If there are sufficient funds in the account the transaction is authorised, the cash is dispensed and the account balance is updated straight away.

The wide availability of ATMs has both advantages and disadvantages. You could be asked to give or choose some of these in the examination.

For the advantages some possible answers are:

- banks can keep their operating costs down because fewer employees are needed to work behind the counter inside branches;

- customers have 24-hour access to their accounts seven days a week;

- there's no need to carry a large amount of cash around, as the large number of ATMs means it is readily available.

For the disadvantages some possible answers are:

- bank employees could lose their jobs;

- criminals can withdraw money from accounts by watching people enter their PIN numbers and then stealing their cards.

TIP

Cheque clearing

Once a cheque has been written and paid into the bank, a process called **clearing** begins: this describes the steps that take place in order for the correct amount of money to be transferred from the account of the person who wrote the cheque to the account of the person whose name is written on the cheque. Cheques are processed using **MICR** (this was described in Chapter 3). The stages of the clearing process are described below. They take from three to five days to complete on average.

- The amount written on each cheque is entered by hand and printed at the bottom of the cheque in **magnetic ink**;

- All of the cheques that have been paid in that day are sent to a central processing centre called a **clearing house**;

- The data printed at the bottom of the cheque in magnetic ink is automatically input by passing the cheques through magnetic ink **character readers**, transferred onto magnetic disk and sorted into bank order. MICR is used because data from large numbers of cheques can be input very quickly and accurately;

- All the data for each bank is copied onto individual magnetic disks;
- All the cheques are sorted into bank and branch order and sent back to each bank, where they are stored in case there are any problems or enquiries from customers;
- A magnetic disk containing a **transaction file** (with details of all the amounts to be added to and deducted from customer accounts) is sent to the bank's own computer centre;
- Customer accounts are updated using the transaction file.

Electronic funds transfer

All banks offer their customers the use of a **debit card** facility. **MAESTRO** (previously **SWITCH**) and **DELTA** are the two main types of debit card in the UK. These cards can be used instead of cash or cheques. This type of payment system is called **electronic funds transfer** or just **EFT** for short; its main advantages are that bank accounts are updated straight away and there's no need to use cash or wait for cheques to clear. Suppose, for example, you were paying for a CD in a music store using a debit card. Your card would be swiped through a magnetic stripe reader and your bank's computer would be contacted to make sure there was enough money in your account to pay for the CD. Provided that the funds were available, the payment would be authorised and the money would be exchanged electronically between the shop's computer and your bank account.

Smart cards

A smart card looks exactly like a credit or debit card except that it has a microchip built into it which can be used to store much more data than a magnetic stripe, more reliably and securely. Money is transferred directly from the customer's bank account using special telephones or ATMs, and stored on the card inside an "electronic purse". To use the card it must be unlocked using a PIN. Retailers have a special terminal which has their own smart card inside. When goods or services are purchased the customer's card is placed in the terminal and money is transferred from one card to another.

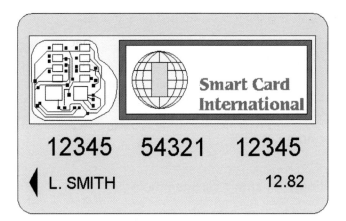

CS4.2 A smart card – the microchip is in the top left-hand corner of the card.

The main advantages of smart cards are:

- they can be used just like cash, without the need to wait for authorisation like EFT systems;
- smart card technology is more reliable than magnetic stripes, which are easily damaged;
- smart cards offer better security than magnetic stripe cards because they are much more difficult to forge, and generate a unique digital code each time they are used.

A single smart card can be used for different applications at the same time, such as:

- a credit card;
- an identity card;
- an electronic key to open doors that have been fitted with locks that have smart card readers fitted;
- a bureau de change, by holding foreign currencies in extra electronic purses.

Questions

1. (a) What do the letters **EFT** stand for? (1)

    (b) Give **one** method of input used by an EFT system. (1)

    (c) Give **two** advantages of using an EFT system. (2)

    (d) Give **one** disadvantage of EFT. (1)

2. Many banks are experimenting with smart card technology.

    (a) What is a **smart card**? (2)

    (b) Give **three** advantages of smart cards compared with traditional magnetic stripe card technology. (3)

3. Every bank in the country has a network of cash machines, or ATMs.

    (a) Give **two** input devices used at an ATM. (2)

    (b) Give **two** output devices used at an ATM. (2)

    (c) To use an ATM a customer needs a debit or credit card and a PIN.

    (i) What do the letters **PIN** stand for? (1)

    (ii) Explain why a **PIN** is needed. (1)

    (d) Give **three** services, other than withdrawing cash and checking account balances, you would expect a typical ATM to offer customers. (3)

Web tasks

1. Read Reynolds Griffith's article "Cashless Society or Digital Cash?" at:
    www.sfasu.edu/finance/FINCASH.HTM

2. Write your own argument about whether we will ever have a truly 'cashless' society and the impact this might have on our lives.

    You may also find these links useful:
    www.networkusa.org/fingerprint/page5a/fp-05a-page5a-cashless.html
    www.heise.de/tp/english/special/eco/6093/1.html

Index